GAINING TRACTION

A BEGINNER'S GUIDE TO PRODUCT MANAGEMENT

THOMAS **RAFFAEL**

DEDICATION

This book is dedicated to my grandfather, Maurice Raffael, from whom I had hoped to learn so much.

CONTENTS

Acknowledgments   i

How to Read This Book   3

1   What Is a Product Manager?   5

PART ONE: RESEARCH

2   Product Strategy: The Basis of Every Decision   10

3   Understanding Your Customers   21

4   Research Techniques   31

PART TWO: DESIGN

5   UX Design: The Basics   48

6   Minimum Viable Products: Where It All Starts   57

7   UX Design: Further Points   64

PART THREE: EVERYDAY WORKING

8   Why You (Mostly) Want to Avoid Waterfall   84

9   Transitioning to Continuous Development   89

10 How to Say No (or Sometimes Yes!)   94

11 Stakeholder Management   98

12   How to Deal with Bugs   103

13   Feature Bloat: Why Features Sometimes Aren't the Answer   113

14   Time Management   116

15   Sprint Planning and Retrospectives   124

16   Your Product Roadmap   129

17   How to Prioritise Product Development   132

18   Working with a Remote Dev Team   139

PART FOUR: TOOLS

19   Google Analytics: The Basics   144

20   Intercom: Your Secret Weapon   162

PART FIVE: SKILLS

21   SEO: An Introduction   176

22   Technical SEO   181

23   Off-Page SEO   198

24   On-Page SEO   203

25   Introduction to Behavioural Psychology   219

26   Introduction to HTML, CSS and Javascript   239

Epilogue   250

Glossary   252

Further Reading   255

References   256

ACKNOWLEDGMENTS

A few people have been critical in preparation for this book. First of all, thank you to Richard Skinner, who has taught me much of what I know. Thank you to Adam Price for getting me started in Product Management. Thank you to Caroline Lund and Joao Martins, who have added their professional two cents to some chapters. Thank you to Neil Patel, Vincent Dignan, Nir Eyal and Intercom for granting me permission to use some of their graphics. And a big thank you to Clare Hogg, my mother, for helping to edit this book.

How to Read This Book

Product Management is a wide field. You need to know everything from the principles of behavioural psychology to the details of CSS.

This book is a beginner's guide to it all. You, who are reading this book, probably have at least some of the skills and knowledge explained here so feel free to dip in and out of the parts which most apply to you.

If you are a complete beginner, there is no better place to start than this book. Read it cover to cover and once you have, I have included at the end of this book a list of other books which I would recommend. You can never learn enough in product management – a field which is developing at an accelerating rate.

My personal experience

I have written this book with an emphasis on web-apps because that is my expertise. The main lessons all apply for mobile apps too and even where a topic is web-specific like SEO, you will likely end up with a website version of your app or have landing pages you want to rank in Google or have a company blog you will want to optimise.

Common examples

Before I became a product manager, I started developing a website called FoodZube, which is a recipe planning and delivery web-app. Although only half built, I use it in hypothetical examples throughout this book to avoid being seen to critique another company's product.

I also provide real life examples of my time at VouchedFor, a platform which helps people find the best legal and financial advice, and which is already improving the standards of these professions.

Overall

Please enjoy the book!

1

What Is a Product Manager?

This is a question you will be asked at dinner parties and never know how to answer.

I've tried "I work in tech" and "I design websites", the first of which is vague and the latter not quite true.

A product manager is the glue between the technical side (coding and designing) and the rest of the business. You could be referred to as the product 'CEO' and as such, you should be able to put yourself in the shoes of nearly anyone at the company – marketing, sales, customer service, developer, UX researcher, designer – because you can't design a good product strategy without thinking about its effect on the rest of the business. Your product is being promoted by the marketing team and supported by the customer service team. Any change you make to your product may require a change of strategy for them.

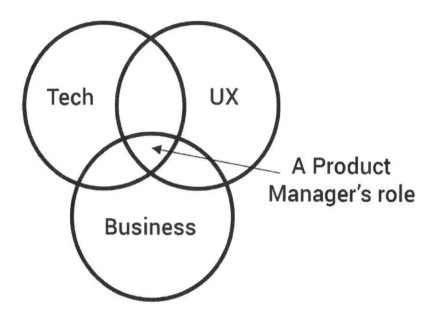

Inspired by Mind The Product's famous Venn diagram

You will translate business goals for the tech and design teams.

When there is a skills gap in your team, it will likely be you who needs to fill it.

In teams I have been in, there often hasn't been a UX (user experience) researcher, a UX designer or a UI (user interface) designer. Many times, there was no product marketing manager and no business development manager. It will be up to you to get the job done.

Your responsibilities will likely include most of the following:

- Task prioritisation
- Product research
- Product design
- Product scope
- Product performance and analysis
- Product strategy (strategy for any time period from the next quarter to the next five years)

In other words, you are responsible for what to build and delivering it, but mostly not the technical details of how it gets built (that's for your developers and designers).

You lead the product team, but curiously, no-one reports to you. You will need to influence people rather than direct them. You are the leader of a team who all work together on the same goal.

I've found that this curious position is a help. No-one feels they *have* to do something for you but you are all there to reach the same goal. This equality means the team can gel and team members feel free to speak their mind to you, which is hugely important.

PART ONE: RESEARCH

2

Product Strategy: The Basis of Every Decision

A product strategy is the basis of every decision you make with your product. With one, you have a great chance of reaching your goal. Without one, you are building your house on sand.

In your product strategy, you need to answer the following questions in the following order:

1. What job does your product do and who for?

2. What kind of product is it?

3. How will you know it's doing that job?

4. What are the key components that will enable it to do

that?

5. What makes you uniquely positioned to create that product?

6. Who else is competing to do this job?

7. Who can you be inspired by?

Create a strategy document with these sections. Keep it to two pages – no-one will read it if you don't. Provide a slide deck to go with the document outlining your conclusions in a more visual way. The document provides the in-depth answers while the slide deck gives the high-level story.

Once you have some experience with product strategy, you can write it in any format you like. It could be a mind map, a poster on the wall that you write all over, or any format that captures the points you've got and can be easily communicated to your audience.

Start from first principles

Get rid of your biases and beliefs and ask yourself the most dangerous question:

"Should my product even exist?"

Ask this question even if your product is mature because it helps you think more creatively about solutions. Product managers can get so wrapped up in the detail that it is hard to see the big picture.

I'm going to answer the question with my hypothetical food

app, FoodZube, which does your grocery shopping for you.

"Yes, it should exist because people need an easier way to organise their grocery shopping."

Do they though? Aren't people eating more ready meals now? And aren't the people who do buy groceries doing fine with the system they use right now?

This train of thought helps expose your assumptions. Keep challenging yourself to find all the assumptions you need to test and the kind of questions you need to answer.

What your product does and who it's for

You likely have an idea for a product in mind, but remain open-minded. Start with your target market. Use secondary research from think-tanks or internal company research to get an idea of who your target market could be. If your product already exists, your current customers are likely (but not necessarily) your target market.

Here are the questions to answer about your target market:

- What do they want?

- What do they *need?*

- What is currently causing them strife?

- How are they currently solving the problem?

- What might stop them moving to a new solution?

To answer these questions, speak to people in your target

market. Interview them, organise focus groups, go into wider market research – there's more on this in Chapters Three and Four.

In your interviews, ask questions like:

- When you're doing <activity x>, which part is the most difficult? (for B2C customers)
  - What is something if you had a magic wand you would change about <activity x> right now?
    - How do you deal with that now?
- What niche are you in (for B2B customers)?
  - What is your main driver of growth? (get to know as much as possible about their business)
- What is something that you do every day that you hate doing in your business? (for B2B customers)
  - What is something if you had a magic wand you would change in your business right now?
    - How do you deal with that now?
- When do you normally use <competitor product name/alternative solution>?
  - Sometimes this question can mean 'at what time of the day' – getting an idea of where your product can fit into your customer's everyday life is important context.

Have a conversation with your customers rather than rattle off a list of questions. Inquire further after an initial answer to gain insight below the surface. Sometimes a Five Whys approach can be helpful to get to root problems or causes (see more about the Five Whys in Chapter 12).

If your product already exists, you will want to see customers using your product.

You can also ask questions more specifically about your product right now:

- What problems do you have with <business/product name>?

- How do we help your life (B2C)/business (B2B) today?

As well as customers, talk to your colleagues – they're the most readily available source of knowledge. Ask them some basic questions:

- What problems do our customers have with us today?

- What problems do we have when we try to help our customers?

- What makes us uniquely positioned to help our customers?

- What problems do we solve for our customers?

- Where do you see <product name> going in the next year?

At VouchedFor, I did these interviews in small groups of 3-5 in a similar way to my sprint retrospectives (see more on those in Chapter 15).

I gave everyone some post-it notes and for each question, I asked them to write their answers – one answer per post-it. Then I would go round the table and ask people to read out their answers.

I put the post-its on the wall in front of us, grouped into themes. We would discuss what people meant by some of their ideas and comments and then I would take a photo of the wall before we moved onto the next question.

Only once you have done your research can you decide what job your product should do for your target market. This should be high-level e.g. "We should create a product to help people sort their finances out".

Type of product

Once you know the job your product should do, you can work out where it fits into people's lives. Is it a product for daily use? Or one that will be used once during a particular life event, for example?

The answer to this question will change how you design the app and which features you prioritise.

Evaluating product performance

It will be important to track how well your product is doing its job.

Engagement and retention rates are important metrics to measure for daily use products. Life event products (e.g. getting a mortgage) can focus more on conversion and promotion (i.e. how many people who used your product recommended it to a friend).

Because you are developing your app all the time, it is important to measure this by monthly cohort (more on this in Chapter Four).

Key product themes

These are the themes to focus on in the year ahead to achieve your vision (or get as close to it as possible in the timeframe). For each theme, you should show the research which makes clear why you have chosen this theme for your year-long strategy.

For a business like FoodZube, a theme might be "Manage diets easily" or it could be something more technical like "A new CMS" (Content Management System). You'll want to outline your solution but it should be no more than an outline. For example, with diets, your suggested solution may be a 'diet dashboard' where you can view your diet progress and change your recipe filters, but you don't go into detail.

Your unique market position

Set out what you believe are your unique selling points and what is stopping others doing the same thing (i.e. barriers to entry).

For example, VouchedFor made a 'free financial plan' product, which they were uniquely able to do due to their status as the middle man between a large pool of financial advisers and advice seekers. They were able to research what both sides needed from such a product, with readily available interviewees and a large quantity of data. Few others had the position in the market to create a product right for both parties.

Market & Competitors

With a grocery delivery app, there are multiple competitors. Firstly, there are the other grocery delivery apps available. But they are actually only a small minority of your competitors.

Every supermarket is a competitor and every restaurant is a competitor because people are looking for solutions, not apps.

Their problem is that they are hungry. Maybe even their garden is a competitor to your app.

In your product strategy document, write a list of your competitors and separate them out into direct (other grocery apps) and indirect (restaurants) competitors. Find out their strengths and weaknesses and work out what your space in the market can be.

This section is where to provide information on market size, growth and other market research.

Inspiration

Find products that are not direct competitors but can be indirect competitors. Sometimes, they can be in completely different markets – think about the number of products influenced by Uber or Tinder, for example.

There is little new in the world. Someone has probably done something similar to your idea before. It's worth finding out what happened and what lessons can be learnt.

Other product themes

If your product is mature, you may need to concentrate on some technical themes.

For example, on one of the products I was managing, I knew there was a problem with the number of bugs that popped up. I did analysis on the bug reports coming into our Trello[1] board to find out where the bugs were coming from and why. I created a report in Jira to see what percentage of our tasks were bugs in the last two quarters. At the end, I had findings on why we got bugs, how to deal with them and evidence to show that this was a theme for my product area to tackle in the coming year.

The product vision

If your product (or product area) doesn't already have one, it is worth articulating a vision so you have a goal to reach. This provides structure for your product development and lets colleagues understand your product better.

After research and conversations with upper management, you can focus on the vision. The best vision statements make themselves clear through your research and you merely have to articulate it. For example, FoodZube's vision statement is:

"Make healthy cooking easy for everyone"

Here are some others:

Nike: To bring inspiration and innovation to every athlete in the world.

Microsoft: Create experiences that combine the magic of software with the power of Internet services across a world of devices.

Google: To organize the world's information and make it universally accessible and useful.

These are business vision statements, not individual product visions but they follow the same principle: a product vision should never be fully attainable. There should always be more you can do to get closer to reaching your vision.

But only create a product vision if you are going to be a visionary – if you mean it and want to bring your colleagues with you. If you are making one just for appearance's sake, it won't help you.

Once you have your vision set, you have an anchor from which to base all future decisions. You know where you want to go.

***

I prefer to keep a product strategy to a year in a startup environment – any longer than that and the strategy is in danger of becoming irrelevant. More stable business or product environments can have strategies for much longer periods.

Conclusion

A product strategy is your reference point for everything you build. It focuses you on reaching your vision. If someone in the business wants to change the direction of your product, they need to provide a very good case for why their suggestion is a greater priority than the well-researched strategy which has already been agreed upon by all managers and stakeholders.

3

Understanding Your Customers

Your customers are your ultimate boss.

It's not your manager, not the CEO and not the shareholders; your ultimate boss is your customers. Because if your customers don't like your product, they will fire it without the slightest twinge of sympathy. They pay the bills and always will, so the most important part of your job is to understand them.

In the best scenario, you are one of your own customers. If not, get into the shoes of your target customer. There are two types of customer: potential customers who have not yet bought your service or product and actual customers who have.

Potential customers

Your potential customers' lives have nothing to do with your product. Your product shouldn't be formulated until you hear about them.

When conducting research with potential customers, the conversation needs to be open-ended. You can't lead your customers down a certain line of thinking.

Here's a bad way to approach a conversation with a potential customer:

You: Do you like cooking apps?

Them: Yeah, I've heard some great things about ___

You: Great, well we've got this great new cooking app coming out next month. It does X, Y and Z. Would you be interested?

Them: Wow, I've always wanted X, how come no-one's done that before?

You: I know, right? So do you think you would be willing to pay £X for it?

Them: Yeah probably. Let me know when you're ready to launch.

You: Absolutely!

Off you go, happy as a lamb! You've just signed up a new customer! You'll go back to the office and tell everyone the good news. But here's what actually just happened:

You: Do you like cooking apps? Leading question. You haven't found out anything about how your target customer lives his life yet.

Them: Yeah, I've heard some great things about ___ He means: Well, I haven't actually used one before, but I heard about one which sounded kind of cool for someone who does use cooking apps.

You: Great, well we've got this great new cooking app coming out next month. It does X, Y and Z. Would you be interested? It's pretty hard for this target customer to say no without being rude. And you're giving solutions before you've even heard the problems.

Them: Wow, I've always wanted X, how come no-one's done that before? Notice he doesn't actually say 'Yes I am interested'. Also he says he's always wanted X, so are you going to ask him what he's done to get X or what his workaround has been so far?

You: I know, right? So do you think you would be willing to pay £X for it? No, you're not, it seems. You'd prefer to pat your-self on the back. Of course, this is much too early to talk about price because you know nothing yet. Then giving him a price to accept gives him a lot of pressure. He knows you won't ask for payment right now, so he's free to lie to keep things cordial.

Them: Yeah probably. Let me know when you're ready to launch. He means: I have a passing interest in what you're doing and I don't want you to feel bad, so tell me how it goes, but I'm probably not interested.

You: Absolutely!

So in a month's time, when you launch, and your target customer doesn't sign up and everyone in the office asks what happened, you'll think it was bad luck. You and your business won't have learned anything. Your job is to learn. You need to understand how your customer lives his life and then try to come up with a way to make his life easier that he'll really want. So a good start to a conversation with your potential customer should go more like this:

You: Take me through your weekly routine. When do you get back from work? How many days do you work?

Them: I work 5 days a week and I normally get back around 7pm. I go for a 20 minute jog. Then I cook something small for myself in the evening while watching my favourite TV series. I'll usually go to bed around 11pm and wake up at 7.

You: What about the weekends – do you cook then too?

Them: No, I'm out most of the day with friends. We'll get something in the pub in the evening.

You: So during your working week, how do you decide what to cook?

Them: I have some recipe books I flick through but most of the time I just try to use up leftovers in my fridge. When I buy new food, I always look for things I can freeze.

And so the conversation goes on. You are not there to pitch your product, you are there to find out what they need your product to be! Let's have a look at that conversation again:

You: Take me through your weekly routine. When do you get

back from work? How many days do you work? Asking an open-ended question to start off means you can get a feel for this person's life. Each person will answer differently and give you different types of useful information. If they go too far off course, your next question may need to lead them back to your area (in this case, cooking).

Them: I work 5 days a week and I normally get back around 7pm. I go for a 20 minute jog. Then I cook something small for myself in the evening while watching my favourite TV series. I'll usually go to bed around 11pm and wake up at 7. You've learnt so much! Presuming this person represents your target market, you've learned a lot about who they are. They care about their fitness and health. They cook just for themselves (so do they live alone? Do they have a family? – questions to ask!). They like to watch a TV series while they eat (worth suggesting a good TV series to watch in your cooking app? Might be worth investigating). It seems they do this every evening, but it's worth clarifying that later.

You: What about the weekends – do you cook then too? You've noticed they only mentioned their working week, so it's time to ask another open-ended question.

Them: No, I'm out most of the day with friends. We'll get something in the pub in the evening. Hmm, ok. So if your cooking app is mainly for their working week, maybe best not to include a solution for the weekend. Or maybe a way to develop your app further down the line. Either way, you can make a more informed decision on the direction and design of your app now.

You: So during your working week, how do you decide what to cook? Now we're going into detail. Do they have any problems with how they cook right now? Is there a problem to be solved?

Them: I have some recipe books I flick through but most of the time I just try to use up leftovers in my fridge. When I buy new food, I always look for things I can freeze.

- So they care about cooking enough to own some recipe books, but they don't use them much. Why not? That's worth knowing.
- They like to avoid wasting food. Why is that primarily? Is it because they're short of money? If so, it's worth noting that when deciding the price. Is it because they feel morally obliged to not waste food? Or more specifically because they want to be friendly to the environment? Worth finding out (in an open-ended way).
- Also, the fact that they freeze their food is a very useful piece of information. So do they cook in large batches and eat the same meal the next day or next week? Are they doing this primarily to save money?

In just this small exchange, you have learnt so much and you have so many more questions to ask. And you need to ask all these questions before trying to build a solution to a problem you

a) Don't know people have
b) Don't know if it's a big enough problem for people to pay good money for a solution

Ideally, once you've got to know them well, you would try to live for a while like your target customer or if you're in the B2B space, depending on the context, you may want to ask if you can shadow your target customer on their day-to-day life to get a real feel of the real friction points in their professional life.

Actual customers

I was lucky. I started out in sales and customer service. I was on the phone with customers and potential customers every day before I moved into product in the same company. I had my finger on the pulse of customer thoughts and demands more than anyone else at the company at the time. Having this experience put me a great position to move into product management.

I was also lucky in another sense. Toward the end of my time in sales, the team was growing rapidly. A few months into my time as a product manager, there was a team of salespeople who were doing a lot of my user research for me. We used a CRM to categorise feedback based on different calls and actions and every email we received was categorised with a tag, so it was easy to see a certain type of feedback.

Spend time with your sales team

If you are a product manager in a company which also has a sales or account management team, it is worth spending time with them. Even sitting at the next desk, you will overhear conversations that can highlight a specific problem or customer need. Often, the sales team will use headsets and you'll be able to plug in a second headset so you can listen into conversations for insight.

Other times, you'll want to take some emails and calls yourself and get back into the daily action of sales. This gives you a good understanding of what is going on everyday when you may have spent more time in meetings or speaking with your developers.

Make your CRM useful

If used correctly, CRM systems can be very useful. Firstly on a side note, choose a free one unless you have a very big team, and keep it simple. If you want more than basic CRM functionality, you need to really ask why it's necessary because every time you complicate your CRM, the harder it will be to use and maintain. There's little basic functionality that Salesforce, the expensive market leader, can do that SuiteCRM cannot, for example. But SuiteCRM can fall over if too much custom functionality is added.

It's worth keeping a record of the types of calls being made and the outcomes of them in a way that can be read as statistics. Having plain text call logs is important for the qualitative part of the analysis, but dropdown lists to categorise a call and its outcome are equally important. You will be able to see numbers downgrading and why. You will be able to see the number of potential customers turning into real customers and why some potential customers don't want to sign up. There is a wealth of information at your fingertips if you structure your CRM right.

Meet your customers

But nothing beats meeting your customers in person. Startups don't meet their potential customers partly because it may mean meeting them on the street and face rejection most of the time and partly because there's always something 'urgent' that has to be done. It's amazing how things keep on going when even the CEO is on holiday for a week – maybe those 'urgent' things can wait and we can go and meet our customers.

AirBnB is a good example of a company who tried to be scalable with technology without meeting customers. They struggled for months before they decided to fly around the United States and meet their customers.[1] On their travels, they heard hundreds of stories and with the data points they collected, they figured out a better way to scale.

I have certainly found that the times I have had lunch with one of our customers or gone to their offices to see how they work (if I'm working B2B) have been the times I have learnt the most about how to serve their needs the best.

Conclusion

When you join a new company, the first thing you should do is get to know the company and its customers inside out. You need to use all the tools available to you: your sales team (if there is one), your other colleagues (to give you their unique insight), your CRM, the email support system and, of course, conversations with your customers.

When you want to understand what your customers need, the problem must come first and not your proposed solution. You must be willing to see that your solution may not be the right one and re-think what the right one is, if there is even a need for a solution to that particular problem.

4

Research techniques

Now it's time to go into more detail about how to understand your customers.

For any product you develop, you'll need to conduct research before and during development. You will undertake some big research projects and you will be engaged in continuous discovery. In continuous discovery, research happens in your sprints so you can react fast. This will keep your product always responsive to customer needs.

Different research techniques fit certain phases of development especially well. The table below shows the techniques which fit well for each phase.

	Development phase		
	Strategy - what to make?	**Design - how to make it?**	**Assessment - how's it performing?**
Types of questions to answer	What is the perfect product-market fit? What works best for our customers and our business goals?	Now we know what to build, are we making it in the right way? Are we taking the right approach? This is about structure and design.	Where do we go from here? What does v2 look like? Should we pivot?
Approach	Quantitative and qualitative	Mostly qualitative	Mostly quantitative
Methods	Field studies, surveys, analytics, secondary research	Field studies, usability studies, card sorting, eyetracking studies	A/B testing, customer interaction, analytics, session recording

A note about qualitative and quantitative research

Qualitative research takes you deep into why, where and how people are using your product or user problems which may warrant a solution. On an individual level or in small groups, you can find out about how people tick. But qualitative research is anecdotal, even when done extensively.

Quantitative research doesn't generally answer questions like 'why' – it's often just raw numbers – but it can give you statistically significant data. While you still need to interpret the data, it can tell you what people are *doing* on your app. This is important because there can be a big gap between what people say they do and what they actually do. So quantitative research is behavioural and qualitative is attitudinal.

Field studies

A field study is where you spend time with a member of your target audience/customer to understand her life. Shadow a customer as she takes you through her day or interview her.

When I was researching Finnish schools, I sat at the back of the classroom. After classes, I would informally ask students how they found the lesson, whether they found the iPads included useful and how they used them, for example. I spent a week observing and asking questions after an event or situation.

I have been lucky that the field studies I have undertaken have been free. If you have a broad consumer-based target market, you may want to consider talking to people on the street to keep costs down. Often, people will be happy to talk to you for free or for the offer of a free coffee.

Working in a lean way, you could go out with your entire

team, developers and all, to talk to your target market in the morning, re-design your wireframes/prototypes in the afternoon, and get back in the field the following morning for more feedback.

Field studies show you how your target market live their lives. Without this deep understanding, you can't know what your product should do or who it should be for.

If you are building a food planning app, and your field study shows that your target customer, who is 50 years old, always uses their laptop for food planning, not a phone or tablet, that can drastically change your approach to the way you design your app, for example. If it also shows that your target customer doesn't come back from work until 9pm, that too can change your core product proposal.

Unless you already have experience or expertise in your domain, field studies should always play an important part in the early stages of product research.

Interviews

Normally, field studies come with an interview stage. While the field study is more about observation, interviews are mostly about understanding. The previous chapter covers the basics of the type of questions to ask in interviews.

If you need interviewees to come to the office (which saves time compared with going to them), it's best to leave the organising of this to someone outside the team if possible because this can be time-consuming. Bringing customers or potential customers into the office frequently makes sense if you are iterating quickly.

Focus groups

Focus groups can be more efficient that individual interviews, reaching more of your target audience at one time. The discussion that comes out of a focus group can teach you things that a one-to-one interview cannot.

You can learn what users want from a solution like an app. However, it's more difficult to learn about good interface design from a focus group, which is better done one-to-one. Interacting with an interface is a personal experience and third party opinions are not useful in this setting.

Tips for a successful focus group:

- Before your focus group starts, the group members should have got some background about what your app is about. At the start, you should explain the format of the session and make introductions.
- Make sure to have at least one other team member or another colleague with you for the focus groups – you will want more than your own perspective on what happened.
- Focus group size varies depending on whether you want a broad discussion or a deep one. For broad discussions, larger sizes work best while smaller sizes work for deeper discussions. For deeper discussions, I have found a focus group of five people optimal and

for broader discussions you don't want more than nine – quieter people should not have the opportunity to be shy.

- Focus groups should last not longer than two hours. One hour will often be enough, or less for a small group. If it lasts too long, unless it's a vibrant discussion, members will become less creative.

Sometimes, I have led focus groups as an open discussion. More often, I have used post-it notes to get ideas on paper before the group members can influence each other. Once all the ideas are stuck on the wall, we can have a deeper discussion of these ideas or beliefs and what they mean.

After all the focus groups have been completed, you should listen back to the recording you made, as well as the notes you and your colleagues took. Summarise each meeting and find the common themes.

Surveys

In a survey, you can't ask your questions in such a personal or tactful way like in an interview, and you can't follow up on questions. If you give the options as radio options or tick boxes, you have framed the answer too, when the full truth may be more nuanced than your multiple choice can provide. However, they are often the fastest and cheapest option for getting attitudes on a large scale.

One thing that surveys can be especially useful for is pricing. The results should be taken with a pinch of salt because they measure how people say they will react rather than how they do react (the two can be very different). Nevertheless, they provide a starting point for pricing structure and number.

In the surveys I've undertaken about pricing, I've been surprised at how honest customers have been when answering how much they would be willing to pay. This has been proven by customers' reaction after we changed pricing.

But surveys can be useful for attitudes too – I have used SurveyMonkey Audience to understand people's evening eating habits and problems. Mostly, I used text boxes for people to write their own comments to avoid bias in the answers that radio options can cause. Be careful about this though, because if the survey takes too long and is too tiresome, fewer people will complete it.

Keep your survey simple. People should be able to understand the question and know how to answer it easily.

Customer emails and phone calls

A great, ever-flowing river of insight comes from the everyday interaction with customers. Your inbound customer service emails can be tagged so you can follow certain themes. Phone calls get logged in your CRM, both inbound and outbound, and can be a great source of insight.

This is where you can see why people downgraded or why they never signed up. Often, tagged emails or categorised phone calls are easy to export into a spreadsheet where you can make your own categorisations, as well as seeing the detail of what happened in each case, including the history of the customer.

I have spent time listening into the phone calls of account managers and have done quite a bit of sales and customer service myself. There is no substitute for being involved first hand and speaking with customers in a live situation.

Transactional and marketing emails and in-app messages

If you have Intercom (see Chapter 20), you can turn marketing and transactional emails and in-app messages into one of your most targeted sources of insight.

Feedback forms

On some websites and apps, if someone chooses to cancel or downgrade, you can ask them to state why they are doing it as an optional step.

Alternatively, you can have a feedback form people can always fill in. The image below is an example of a common position of a feedback form – next to the scrollbar on the right hand side of the page, half way down the page.

However, if you have Intercom, this is unnecessary.

Session recording

There are services out there (e.g. Inspectlet) which can record the sessions of your site users. Instead of hearing what people *say* they would do, you can see what people *are* doing.

The main challenge with this type of research is figuring out what people wanted to do. On simple pages, this is clear, but on pages with many options, it's less clear. Nevertheless, most of the time you can really see how people are using your site and why.

Mouse-tracking

A service like CrazyEgg will let you track mouse movement and clicks on every page of your website. Are visitors clicking on something which is unclickable? What did they expect to happen next?

You can see heatmaps of this movement and clicks, which can give you an idea of where people's eyes are moving too without having to set up special equipment.

Mouse-tracking is an important part of measuring your users' user experience.

Search logs

Having a search bar on your app or site can be a great research channel.

If people are searching for something, it means they haven't found it on their current page. If that page has been designed to answer that question, you know the design is off. If users are searching for something you don't have or want information in a different way to how you've set up your site, this is important information too.

Keep a log of searches to make your site more useful. You can set up tracking with Google Analytics or build your own system.

Usability testing

Many interviews come with a usability testing phase. Usability testing is about letting a user experience your product in some form, whether just with wireframes, fully mocked up prototypes or your live app. There are a few different types of usability testing that can come in useful.

Wireframes: Showing your user some wireframes is the fastest and cheapest way of picking up mistakes in layout and sometimes substance. Often, a user will find something missing. For example, doing wireframe testing with users for FoodZube, one user asked "Is there somewhere to specify I only want recipes that can be frozen?" It turned out this user cooked on a Sunday for two weeks worth of meals and would put the meals in the freezer. Earlier research should pick this up but it's better to make this learning at the wireframing stage than after you've launched.

Wireframe feedback is about layout but it's also about imagination. Ask your user where she expects to go if she presses a button or link. If that's not how you imagined it, consider a rethink if that feedback keeps coming up.

Mockups: a full design of the page but not interactive. Mockups largely focus on the style of the page and the feeling the user gets from it. Is it 'likeable'? Clean? Immediately comprehensible?

Prototypes/live site: prototypes are wireframes or mock-ups where the user can navigate across parts of the site like they can on your live site. Whether you are testing with a prototype or your live site/app, this type of testing is about the full experience. Instead of having to imagine the experience like in the wireframe and mockup phases, now the user can give more informed feedback having experienced your app holistically.

Fully mocked up prototypes tend to be the last step before live site/app development – the last opportunity to avoid an expensive mistake before you are committed to coding your feature.

The five-second test: what your page is trying to communicate should be clear within five seconds of the user first setting eyes on it, especially with attention spans so short these days. The five second test is when you show your user a page or app screen for five seconds and then ask them what they thought the page was about and what they remembered from the page. You can do this test at any level from wireframe to live site testing.

A/B testing

A/B testing is simply about testing different variants of a theme in a controlled way. While the name suggests you can test two variants – A and B – you can test multiple variants at the same time. The more variants you add, the longer it will take to get decisive significant data.

A/B testing is not about fundamental questions of structure, substance or design but about optimisation. You may want to test various font sizes or button colours, for example.

I say this not to diminish the value of A/B testing though. EA, the video game company, tested a web page with and without a promotion and found a 43.4% uplift for the variant without.[1]

The type of things you may want to A/B test include:

- Colour
- Position
- Text
- Font size
- Font
- Serif or sans serif
- Videos vs text sales
- Short vs long form copy
- Images
- Fields (for example, in a contact or sign up form)
- Free trial vs money back guarantee vs freemium

Site/app stats

I regularly use SQL from the website database to find data about our user accounts and user behaviour. Google Analytics and Intercom can be helpful here too.

To track progress, you need to view your core metrics by cohort – i.e. a Feb 2016 cohort would be every user who signed up in the month of February 2016. This is important because it shows you the performance of your product as you are developing it.

If you don't use cohort analysis, you can end up with lots of graphs which go up and to the right in a delightful way but give you a thoroughly misleading picture of what's going on. If you are gaining a huge number of signups, but those signups never log in again, they are useless to you (until you can re-engage them). But looking at the number of signups on a graph will make it look like you are in a healthy position.

The core metrics you need to follow will be different for each product, and I would recommend following five or fewer. Some generic core stats which you may wish to consider (all measured as a percentage of the cohort) are:

- Daily active users
- Monthly active users
- Took next best action once
- Took next best action x times
- Paid at least once (i.e. for e-commerce)
- Subscribed
- Retention/attrition within x months

- Advocated product in some way within x months

Other useful non-core metrics to track include:

- Downloads per month (for an app) or signups for a website
- Session length
- Number of sessions per day per user
- Percentage of users with a complaint per month

Conclusion

Before I started out in product management, I used to think that building a successful app or website was about having a great idea that people would naturally swarm to. The thing is, we are a lot more diverse than we think. We like to think that 'people think like me' and that's all the proof you need. But you may not even know yourself that well. Watch carefully and sometimes you think you need a product to make your life better but actually the workaround you've built for yourself is good enough. When that great app you thought you needed finally comes on the market, you sign up, use it once, and then never come back.

For a product manager, research is about knowing your target market better than they know themselves. It's about knowing how people will behave when they don't know themselves, or even give answers that turn out to be wrong upon testing. It's about getting the substance, structure and design right at the earliest stage possible to develop the right solution in the fastest and cheapest way possible.

There are many other research techniques which you may like to take advantage of, like card sorting and diary studies, so make sure to keep up with what's going on. New developments in research and new products and services will become available for you to take advantage of.

PART TWO: DESIGN

5

UX Design: The Basics

In many startups, there may be no UX or UI designer available. It may be up to you to do the job from start to finish with your developer. You therefore need to have a good feel for web design and an ability to wireframe well.

What is UX?

UX means User Experience. UX is concerned about one thing: making sure that your users have the best possible experience on your site or app. Therefore, there are two sides to UX – research and design. All design must be based on research, but there are principles of design to follow after research provides the foundations.

What is the difference between UX and UI design?

UX and UI are different skills. Theoretically, you could have a UX designer who has never used Adobe Photoshop/Illustrator or Sketch in their lives, although this rarely happens. UX design is about providing a good screen layout and user journeys. A UX designer will do wireframes, mock-ups and prototypes. A UI designer will take that basic structure and make it look beautiful.

So, without further ado, what are the main principles of UX design?

Simplicity

In a world of distractions, a simple design is the kindest thing you can do for your customer.

With every element on a page, you must ask:

Is this element helping users reach their goal?

Do you remember Yahoo's home page from 2000? It had everything on there. How about Google's? It had one purpose. Below you can see a case study between Yahoo and Google, where you can see the number of different ways Yahoo draws your attention, which confuses the user and makes it harder for the user to take the action they want to.

Unless you make it absolutely clear what the user's next best action is, many users won't take it.

Any element that is not helping a user reach their goal is hindering them, so delete it.

Taking the examples of forms, at a previous company I worked at, an early version of our registration form was three pages long, with at least ten fields on each page. Reducing this number was a challenge for us because in the industry we worked, a large amount of information was needed for users to get started. But we knew that too many people were dropping out of our registration funnel.

Being ruthless with the information we needed, we reduced our registration form to four fields on one page. There was a second page, but you didn't need to fill it out immediately. You could come back to it.

Through this process and much iteration, we improved the registration funnel completion rate significantly, often being ruthless with which elements we needed on the page at each iteration.

Consistency

To understand the importance of consistency of design, look at the roads.

In the UK, on road signs, motorways are symbolised with a blue background and white text, dual carriageways with a green background and points of interest on a brown background. On all major road signs, the font of the text is the same, the use of capital letters is the same and the symbols for things like roundabouts and t-junctions are the same.

Now imagine that you are on a motorway and all the signs are in green. You might wonder – are you on a dual carriageway? What if the font changed – are you on an official main road or have you got lost? You become insecure and lose trust in the system.

Consistency is important on your site or app too. If the site changes its look, feel and structure on every new page, how are users supposed to get the hang of what's going on? If they can't get the hang of what's going on, how are they supposed to trust your site? And on a separate note, how can you as a business build up a brand that people recognise?

There will be times when you want to A/B test (a topic of Chapter 4) different button colours, for example, and I encourage you to do so. But once your A/B tests come up with a winner, you should stick to the use of that colour on your primary/secondary button design from that moment on (until your entire brand comes up for a change).

So you need a style guide but this guide should only be completed after user research has been undertaken to determine any variables you would like feedback on or need testing.

Standardisation

There is always a temptation when building something new to take the internet/app world to new design boundaries. This can be harmful to you, unless you are a market leader and people will follow you wherever you go (think Apple).

You are not a major player on the internet and when your users are visiting your site or app, you are probably one of ten or twenty sites they've visited that day. If your site works differently to internet norms or differently to norms among your competitors, users are going to have to learn something new. Your site won't be *intuitive*. In a world where your site has five seconds to make a first impression and about as long to make its second, you need to make your site consistent.

This means, for example, that your layout should mirror other major similar sites. If you are an e-commerce site, you may want to follow Amazon's layout, for example. Amazon has spent a huge amount of money running tests, iterating and optimising their product pages. You can use that to your advantage for free.

It also means following other rules. If you are giving a notification message to your users with a red background, it suggests to the user that there's an error. If the background is yellow, it means there is an alert they need to pay attention to. If it's green, it's probably a success message. Follow these intuitive rules to make your app or site as easy to use possible.

Symbols like question marks, crosses and ticks work in the same way. Don't use a new icon to symbolise a common action which has already has an icon everyone connects to it.

Trust

One of the cornerstones of successful UX design is trust. Trust is one of the hardest things to develop between your product and your customers. It's partly why you need to know your users well and it's definitely why you need to make things as simple, consistent and standardised as possible. There is a lot I haven't covered in UX design here, but if you ask yourself 'How can I build up trust with my users through design?', you will find the answers to great UX yourself.

A case study: Google v Yahoo in 2000

Why did Google beat its larger rival Yahoo at the turn of the century? One of the major reasons was UX design. While Yahoo crammed as many things onto its home page as possible, Google did the exact opposite.

This was important for three reasons. Firstly, people knew what to do and weren't distracted from their goal. It looked better, was easier to use and people didn't feel like they were being advertised to.

Secondly, because people didn't feel like they were being advertised to at every opportunity, they had greater trust in Google.

Thirdly, the home page loaded a lot faster on Google than

Yahoo because the page was so clean. In the age of dialup modems, page speed was vitally important.

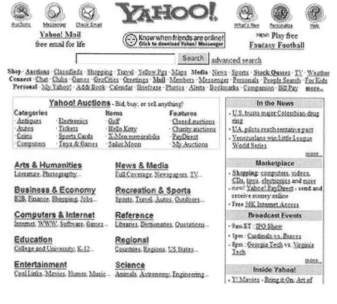

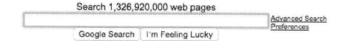

But today, speed is still important. Research by the Aberdeen Group shows that every second counts.[1]

Consequences of a one-second delay

Via NeilPatel.com

Remember, many of your users might be on slow phone connections or on public WiFi. Optimising your site for speed is vital (although be careful of some caching techniques – these can sometimes lead to outdated page screens).

In short, Google looked after its users. They were there to search the internet and they were there for that task alone. Google did everything it could to help them reach their goal.

By contrast, Yahoo saw opportunities to expand their business now they had a lot of traffic coming to it. All their users who were there simply to search the internet found the experience more difficult. When they tried Google, they found it easier and switched.

6

Minimum Viable Products: Where It All Starts

A Minimum Viable Product is the cheapest, smallest experiment you can build which effectively tests demand for your business concept. The experiment is based on user and market research.

I haven't always believed in the concept. I used to think that you should perfect your app before you released it. If you offer customers an under-developed app, they just won't use it. But assuming to know the features to add before you start will lead you to waste money building the wrong features.

If you spend your time building a car when your user is happy with a bike, you've wasted a lot of money. If you're lucky, your user will accept the car. But if the bike would have been more appropriate for him, he may actually be less likely to use your product.

To avoid wasting money and time, you need to create something simple to check you're on the right track.

MVP example

In the following example, you are in the 19th century and your user research has told you a few things:

- That your target users need to get from A to B faster
- That most of them live in cities
- Most of them want to be environmentally friendly
- They are younger, active folk
- They don't have much money

You need to build something cheap that helps people get from A to B faster, can get through horses and carriages fast and doesn't cause any pollution (so horses and their manure are out for the poor city folk who had to smell that!).

The reason you've started asking is because you have a grand concept in your mind that you want validating: a self-powered vehicle that gets you from A to B by just pressing a pedal and using a wheel to steer! That's what you want to build. But you need to curb your enthusiasm and find out the simplest thing people will buy. One step at a time.

The easiest thing to build is probably a skateboard (roads permitting). After launch of your MVP (minimum viable product), the skateboard, you find that your product has gained some interest but your attrition rate is high. After further conversations with your users, you find out that your users are struggling to learn how to use the skateboard. People are losing their balance and falling off; they're also embarrassed to be seen in the streets doing something which looks so preposterous to the 19th Century folk who have seen nothing like this before.

You believe that the two problems are linked: it's hard to look dignified on the street if you're falling off your skateboard all the time and users tended to report both problems together with little feedback about embarrassment by itself. You decide to add a stick and handlebars to your skateboard – this should solve both problems.

After some time, you have enough data to know that this has worked well but you are still struggling to get potential customers interested and your attrition rate remains high.

However, the important thing is that you've proven your business case. There is now clearly enough demand and people are buying your product. You've also found that a small group of customers have got past the initial balancing problems on the skateboard and love the tricks they can do with their boards.

And so your business develops. You may never end up building a car. You may become a skateboard specialist. You may move onto the bike after the scooters you've made for your mainstream customers. Your research may suggest that your customers are now going from A to B fast enough and now have other needs.

Types of MVP

There are a few types of MVP and you will want to choose one based on the type of product you are trying to build – a lot of them don't even involve building even a small product.

- **Video:** the classic example of this is Dropbox. Dropbox is a file storage and syncing system where you can work on a document on your work computer, for example, and save it to your Dropbox 'cloud', then resume work on it on your home computer by opening it from your Dropbox cloud. How do you provide an MVP for something like that? People can either use it or they can't. Dropbox founder Drew Houston tested market demand with a video.[1]

- **Landing page:** many MVPs can just be a landing page. Direct Google, Facebook or any other traffic you like to your landing page and see what demand looks like. This means you don't even need to create a product to test whether it works. Buffer is a good example of a company who did this. They started with a simple landing page with a description of Buffer and a way to express your interest – an email field so you can receive an email when Buffer was ready for launch. After they gauged there was enough interest, they added the element of pricing. How much would people be willing to pay for it? After finding out that with money involved, people were still interested, they created an actual product. A simple one that didn't cost much money to build. This is the process of quick iteration.

- **An actual product:** sometimes the fastest, easiest and most accurate way to gauge interest is by actually putting your product or service out there. AirBnB is a good example of this. Joe Gebbia, co-founder and Chief Product Officer, let a complete stranger stay in his house for free, before realising he could make some money out of this during a 4-day event for designers. His MVP was a simple WordPress website that he set up in a couple of hours. He also used his own house to really experience what his website offers other people.

- **A manual product:** your idea is an automated process to get your customers what they want, right? But automating that process takes time and is expensive. So do everything manually. At VouchedFor, we wanted to test annual pricing, so we called up our customers and asked them if they wanted it. Then we put through annual subscription requests manually.

- **Crowdfunding**: a great way to test early demand is crowdfunding. If people are willing to donate money to make your product a reality, it's probably worth building. You will probably get a lot of useful early suggestions and feedback from engaged supporters.

- **Wireframes/prototypes/designs**: sometimes you can sell your product or service with a simple wireframe or design. Zappos, the shoe retailer, started out with just pictures of the shoes they were going to sell. If you are selling SaaS, wireframes made with Balsamiq may be enough to get early feedback and test demand.

Minimum Lovable Product

A minimum lovable product is an MVP that you are sure will provide a great customer experience.

Some people have offered some resistance to the minimalism of the MVP. They say that the MVP is like putting pieces of metal together with sellotape, adding some wheels quickly and wondering if this will show if your new car can be the next Rolls-Royce. Some MVPs don't take design seriously. As you can see from the different types of MVP above, sometimes they don't have to and sometimes you are offering a service where design isn't important.

But for some entrepreneurs, the MVP needs to look great e.g. for those in the fine jewellery industry. Making the customer feel special can be important too (i.e. their overall experience of your product), not just the way the site looks. So going back to the original example of the skateboard, you may decide to skip the skateboard phase and go straight to the scooter phase if your user research and product tests suggest that this is necessary.

You need to be careful about going too far down this logical path though, because if the skateboard doesn't work, it won't have cost you much and you can then build the scooter. If you build the scooter first, you may miss out on some unexpected interest and learning, as can also be seen from my hypothetical skateboard example.

But sometimes adding a little extra can make the difference – remember your product is your relationship with your customers. As Laurence McCahill, of the Happy Startup School, put it:

"If you go to a hotel room and there's no bed there you'll be a little disappointed, possibly angry. If there's a bottle of champagne, some flowers and a box of chocolates you'll be taken aback and probably over the moon.

What can you do to create a positive response from your customers? Go above and beyond what's expected of you and you'll reap the rewards."[2]

Conclusion

An MVP is what you do after your user research. It is the minimum you need to test demand for your idea. You won't be able to learn everything at this stage, so don't think you'll be able to test your entire business model or plan on a single MVP. You need to iterate quickly and efficiently, in each case testing a single new hypothesis to feel your way through what your users really want. Don't forget that MVPs must work how you expect them to. An MVP can't be an almost working product with lots of bugs. It should be a simple product that works – bugs should not be expected or tolerated in your MVP.

7

UX Design – Further Points

There are some tips in UX design you just won't know about unless someone tells you. Designing a variety of different pages and features for desktop and mobile, I have picked up some of these tips.

Look at what everyone else is doing

Looking at similar types of pages and feature designs to what you want to build can give you the inspiration you need to design your own page. Your best friend here is Pinterest. Other helpful sites include Dribbble, Behance and Google Images.

Web navigation

If your site has more than a few pages, you will need a way to let users easily navigate around the site. This is where category and sub-category pages become useful.

Category pages: these can be based on a task (e.g. contacting a financial adviser), a product (e.g. types of pensions) or a user type (e.g. small business user). Your sub-category pages should have a similar layout to your category pages. These pages are simply about showing users the way to the sub-category or product/service pages on your site in the easiest way possible.

Menu: you should avoid including more than seven items.

Mobile menu: the most common menu in mobile view is a 'hamburger' menu, which looks like this:

This is a fine option but there are two other designs you make like to A/B test:

- Have the word 'MENU' inside a rectangle – this may be more intuitive for users
- Have up to five menu options, represented by icons, available on the screen itself. Facebook has done this, for example.

Search bar: include a search bar – people may want to go a more direct route through your site. The most normal way of designing the search bar is by including the word 'Search'.

Be aware that the length of the search box can also change what people search. Remember to let people press the 'Enter' key to search too.

Navigation bar: keep this simple. This can go along the width of your webpage or down the left hand side. If you go by width, and you have sub-menus, make sure it's easy to click on it. It's very frustrating if there's a sub-menu and your mouse hovers just outside the menu and then the whole menu vanishes.

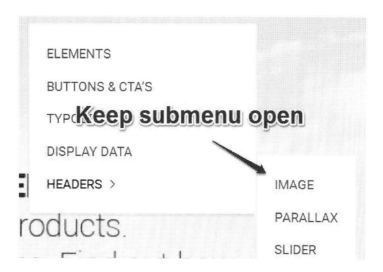

Notifications

This is a pretty easy one.

Red for errors. Yellow for warnings. Green for accomplishments. Blue for important information (although feel more free to use your site's style guide on this one).

And you can get some visually clear ones which pop up with the Javascript plugin Toastr.

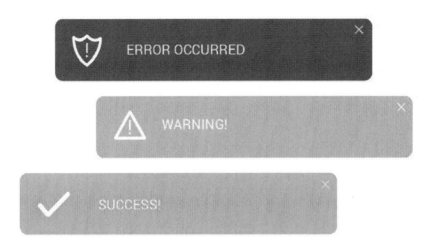

How people read the screen – F and Z

When organising your content on the screen, you should take into account how people naturally read your site.

There are two main ways: reading in an F-shape and a Z-shape.

The F-shape pattern occurs when the page is focused on the text.

The Z-shape example below is a much simpler design than the F-shape example. In the Z-shape, the call to action can and should be the main priority.

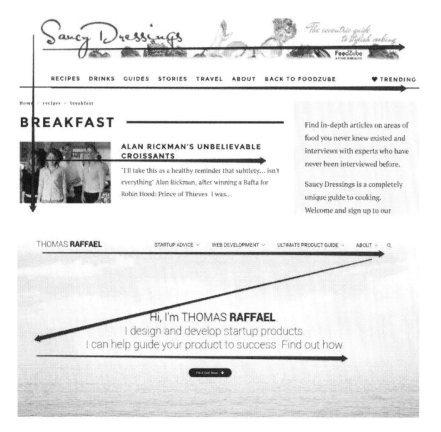

The Z-shape pattern happens when the page isn't full of text.

The different points of the Z are good places for different elements:

- Top left is a good place for your logo
- Top right might be a good place for a search bar – works as a back up call to action if the page doesn't get the user what they want
- Bottom left of the Z is a good place for more information
- Bottom right is where the pattern ends, so your call to action should go here

You can repeat the pattern down the page.

Using mouse tracking software, this can give you an indication of where people's eyes are going. If the trend is not in an F or Z shape, you may want to check other metrics for how well that page is performing – you may have a problem.

Colour blocks

Every page has different sections on it. A simple way to visually show that this is a new section is to give it a new colour. Mostly, pages stick to two alternating colours.

Primary and secondary buttons

Primary buttons should be the most prominent colour in your style guide. They are often the most important feature on the page.

Secondary buttons should be designed to be clear that they are of secondary importance. Many designers don't use a button, but just have links in this role. I think that makes a lot of sense – as soon as you turn a link into a button, it gives it greater prominence, which will take away from your main call to action. If you have several secondary buttons, that can make the page cluttered.

The only thing I would be careful about here is to still make secondary links or buttons large enough to be pressable. There's nothing worse than having links that mobile users find too fiddly to press.

Here are the current designs for FoodZube, although I may move the secondary design to be more links in the future.

Primary button design (+ hover state)

Secondary button design (+ hover state)

The text inside the button should include a verb e.g. Learn; Buy; Contact; Sign up.

One other tip about buttons – rounded edges might perform slightly better. There's a theory that we are conditioned for rounded corners and that they focus our attention on the centre of the button, unlike sharp-edged buttons.

Tooltips

Tooltips are one sentence explainers of a page element.

They can be useful but really they shouldn't be needed. Your design should be self-explanatory enough that they are unnecessary.

However, this isn't always the case. If you need to use tooltips, there are two ways to display them:

- A little icon that can be clicked/pressed. Don't use mouse hover because that only works on desktop. Make sure the icon is a standard one (e.g. an 'i' in a circle) so users can easily recognise it.

- A line of text above, beneath or to the side of the element it refers to. This also makes your tooltip mobile-friendly and makes the information easy to find. You just don't want your tooltip getting in the way of your main user journey. What proportion of users need the tooltip? If it's no more than 10%, you may want to test leaving it out. If more like 40% need the tooltip to know what to do next or feel encouraged, that's a sign your design isn't good enough.

Remember to keep the text in your tooltip short – a simple instructional message should do – and to limit your usage of them.

Modals (overlays/popups)

People call the little window that pops up on the screen a variety of different things – modals, light boxes, popups, overlays – but it's all the same thing.

Use a modal window when you need to draw attention to something and keep your users' attention there. For example, Twitter has one when you want to tweet:

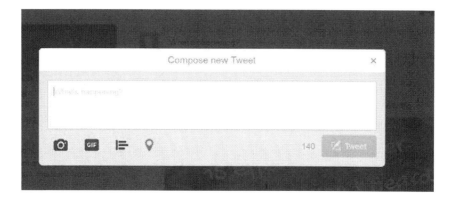

But you need to use modals carefully.

Just like you can't expect people to buy from you the moment they visit your site, you can't expect them to sign up to a newsletter or anything else if they've never seen your site before and haven't yet built up trust. So that means no modals upon site entry – let people see what they came to see.

In general, the rule should be that a modal opens up only upon user action (e.g. clicking a button), but there are two exceptions I would make to this:

- **Interest shown:** if a user has scrolled far down your page or/and has spent some time on it, you can see that they may have a deeper interest in your website and would like to learn more. This can be a good time to offer them that chance. At SaucyDressings.com, I added a modal in exactly this scenario.
- **Exit intent:** if this is a visitor's first session on your site, they've not provided contact details and they

show exit intent with their mouse movement, this is a good time for a modal window. Most people who leave your site will never come back, so providing them with one last great offer (e.g. free expertise) may change their mind.

When you do use a modal there are some things to keep in mind:

- Darken the background – you've taken them to a modal to help the user focus on one action, so make it easy for them
- Let them click out – if they click on the background, that is an intent to go back to the page.
- Have an 'x' in the window – the window should be helping the user, not forcing them to do anything
- Make the 'x' pressable for mobile and tablet – make it big and easy to press
- Keep it simple – anything complex probably warrants its own page

In general, you should use modal windows sparingly. Users often find them annoying and detract from the user experience, as well as from the goal of the page underneath. On mobile, modals have to be full-screen and essentially become a new page which has different navigation rules. If you are going for a mobile-first design, it's best to find another way. Nearly always, there's a good way to have the action in-page rather than in a modal.

Loading screens

The best UX is to have no loading time at all. However, that is sometimes not possible.

Loading ..

Sometimes you eat the bear and
sometimes the bear, well, he eats you.

Slack's loading screen

If you need a loading screen, there are a few principles to stick to:

- Tell users in a visual way how much longer they will have to wait. Defined waiting times feel like they take less time than undefined ones. Progress bars or circles with a 'percent complete' with them are great. An estimated time remaining sentence can be good if accurate.
- Explain the wait. If people know what's loading, they'll be more patient. 'Getting the right results for you' is the type of sentiment you are trying to show.
- Add a personal touch e.g. humour. This can be a good place for your site to show a bit of personality and

connect with your user on a personal level. Slack does this well.

- Educate your users – explain what other awesome features they can use. At FoodZube, on one of our loading screens, I suggest users check out the site's cooking blog or start their own, for example.

Below you can see another of FoodZube's loading screens. We have an animated 'O' and small sentences which move along the screen below which explain the wait:

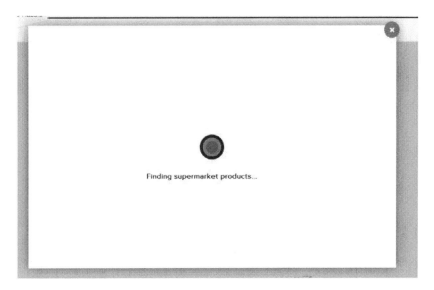

Finding supermarket products...

Confirmation page

When someone has gone through the whole process with you, congratulations is in order! Let them know that they successfully finished the process and what they can look forward to.

The confirmation page is important because it can be the last page in a session for a user. You need them to go away feeling good about themselves and your product.

It's also important because you can use the page as a trigger to start a new product usage cycle.

Here are a few tips for what you can do with this page:

- Cross-sell. They just bought plane tickets. Did they know they can also rent a car on the far side with us?
- Sign them up. If they're going to use your site again, it'll be easier if they save their information so they don't need to type it in again.
  - o Or a newsletter signup may be more appropriate for your product.
- Provide targeted information to help the user with their new purchase. You just bought ingredients for a chicken recipe? Did you know that chicken breasts should be covered with tin foil in the oven to keep it juicy?
  - o There are many variants on this theme but this is a great way to show your users you want to help them wherever you can and you will provide a personalised service for them.
- If your user has just done something cool and exciting, maybe you think you've got a good opportunity of getting your user to share what they've just done/bought on social media!
- Get user feedback. This page is often the best page to get feedback because the process is fresh in the mind.
- Make sure to congratulate the user and make clear the process is over.

Font size, design and line length

Legibility is an art. The fonts you use and how you use them is one of those subconscious factors in how well users can understand your page. There are a few simple guidelines here:

- Bigger font sizes do better on desktop and mobile – 16 pt or higher on desktop. 14 pt on mobile.[3]
- Keep lines of text short – 10-12 words per line on desktop or 7-8 words per line on mobile. Shorter lines are easier to read because of our short attention span.
- Keep some contrast in the colours – calm greys are hard to read on mobile when outside – but I mostly opt for a dark grey over pure black as black can look a bit amateur and be difficult to read for dyslexic users.[4]
- Serif vs. sans serif – I've experimented with the effect of one over the other and found that it doesn't seem to make much difference. Other experiments have also been inconclusive.[5]
- Whatever font you choose (that hopefully fits your brand!), make sure it's easy to read.

Forms

Fields and a 'Submit' button – how hard can it be?

It is pretty easy actually, but there are some tips for a more optimised experience:

- Make the field size appropriate to the amount of in-formation needed. This acts as a visual guide.

- Show users which fields are optional, rather than showing which are compulsory. Users will fill out more fields when you show which fields are optional.[6] This makes psychological sense – if you're told 'fill this in, fill this in and this field', those are the fields you will fill in and you will probably ignore the rest.
- Encourage the user after they have filled in a field correctly with a tick. It's like the site is helping the user on the way and the user will build up trust right from the beginning.
- Keep forms short – which information do you *really* need right now? The smaller the commitment, the more likely the user will finish the form.
- Avoid 'Confirm email' or 'Confirm password' fields unless you are in a high security domain.
- Don't use the word 'Submit' as your call to action in your button but try to use a more descriptive verb to show what will happen next like 'Sign up' or 'Send'.

Pricing pages

The most important factor in a successful pricing page is simplicity. People skim, they don't read. A variation on the '5 second test' – a 10 second test – would give you a good idea of how intuitive your page is.

The pricing page is a good place to keep a standardised design. The same structure of pricing page can be found on sites and apps across the internet. If your product has multiple pricing plans, your page should look something like this:

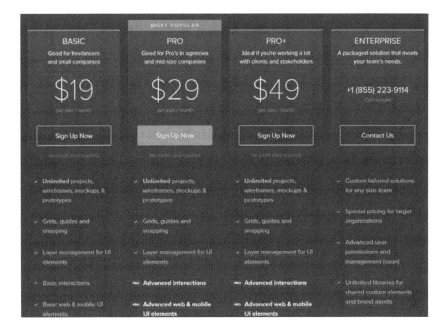

From UXPin.com

In each column, you should have:

- The plan name – this should be descriptive (e.g. 'Premium' and not 'Lightning' or something too creative)
- A sentence about who the plan is for
- The price
- CTA (call to action) buttons with text and tone tailored to the type of people who use the plan most (e.g. a more informal style for younger B2C customers)
- Bullet points (or ticks) with the features of the plan

It should be easy to compare pricing plans. You will want to show users what they don't get as well as what they do get, so grey out and put a strike through any features not included but which are included in other plans. List the features which all plans have first before the features which some plans don't.

Make sure to put the pricing plans in order – most expensive to least expensive or vice versa. On mobile, follow this same order down the page instead of left to right. You may not want to include a free plan if you have one. If the free plan is a last resort for your product to stop users leaving completely, you don't want anyone flocking to that plan when they first arrive.

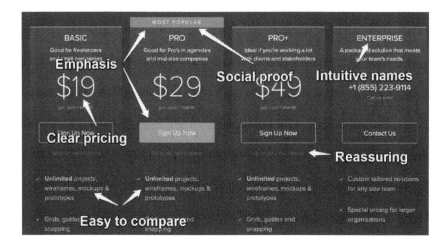

Once you've got the plans in the right order, make sure to highlight the one you most want users to go for. A 'Most popular' or 'Highly recommended' message can be helpful here, as well as visually highlighting the plan. Lifting it above the other plans and changing the colour of the CTA button are other ways of highlighting a plan.

At the bottom of the page, make sure to have an FAQs section. Don't use an accordion (answers are hidden until you click on the question and the answer drops down) here - the answers should be visible. As always when people are serious about buying, they have questions, so make it easy as possible to get the answers.

That means that you should also have a live chat feature on the page so people can ask you questions. This will let you know where the page fails to clarify certain points.

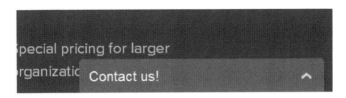

And remember to take the risk away – a money back guarantee or free trial period (especially where no credit card details are required straight away) can greatly increase conversion on your pricing page.

Closing thoughts

All the tips and suggestions mentioned in this chapter are just that – suggestions. They are a good place to start but everything still needs testing. Nothing is universally true in UX design and every target market reacts in a different way to design, so keep speaking to your customers and keep testing.

If you are looking to go down the UX design route as a speciality, it's worth going on a course. There are lots of little details that can make a big difference, like the importance of making a button look clickable, for example. There are more than I can mention here, so please immerse yourself in the subject.

The main tip I would give is to keep looking at Dribbble and Pinterest for inspiration and to see where design trends are going. If you follow the main principles of consistency, standardisation, simplicity and experimentation, you have a good basis for a strong career working in UX design.

PART THREE: EVERYDAY WORKING

8

Why You (Mostly) Want To Avoid Waterfall

Waterfall is a software development method.

The process works in a linear way. Once one phase of development is complete, you can only go forward to the next phase. You can't go back. Hence the name 'waterfall'.

- idea phase
  - plan
    - wireframe
      - design
        - code
          - test
            - deploy

Each phase leads naturally to the next. While it may be the most obvious way to develop an app, it can also be the most wasteful.

A lot of people believe that building an app is simple. You write your code and it works how you designed it. Programming languages are logical, so it can't go wrong. If these statements were true, Waterfall would be more reliable but still wasteful. Even the biggest companies like Apple and Microsoft, after vast amounts of testing and employing some of the best developers in the world, have bugs in their products, so yours will too.

With Waterfall, you start with a project you want to release and you plan the entire project before it gets underway. Once it's started, there's no going back to the drawing board and no stopping a bug being released.

My Waterfall experience

When I first started out in product management, I would write scopes in a Google doc. It would be a few notes and a wireframe. Mostly, it turned out that the detail wasn't enough. I hadn't factored in edge cases or scenarios which led to a poor experience for some of our most important customers. When the developer coded it and released to our testing environment (often referred to as QA or staging), the glaring holes in the scope document became obvious. Some things were so obvious that I thought I didn't need to write them. I assumed the developer would use what I felt was 'common sense' and know the implications of what I had written.

This happened a few times and soon I became more paranoid. I spent longer on the scope documents, knowing as soon as I signed it off, I couldn't take it back – my mistakes would be there for everyone to see.

The scope docs grew in size – first 2 pages, then 4, then 8, then 16 until one day I ended up with a 25 page doc for a white label site. I tried to scope out an entire new website with a variety of complex rules in a single document.

As the number of bugs in the code piled up, more managers needed to co-sign off my scope documents before they went to the developers. Managers who had their own challenges to deal with were supposed to take time out of their schedules to spot the gaps in the detail of the 25 page document I had written.

Once two managers had signed off my scope doc, it finally went to the developers to build. But the code was still buggy and the scope docs still lacked all the detail required, or worse, some detail conflicted with other scope documents.

The result of flawed scope documents and the flawed code based on them was that it took a long time before a project was in releasable state. After release to our live environment, we would find many more bugs than we had anticipated. Since product managers and developers are expensive for a business, this became a major problem.

Morale was down and people assigned blame. Sometimes I would fairly get the blame because my scopes were insufficient. Sometimes the dev team (at this time, product managers and developers were not part of the same team) would get criticism.

And I became so paranoid that I started to map out all of the dependencies of one feature on another and of one webpage on another. I made a matrix which mapped out the entire site and it became clear that there were dependencies all over the place. Taking them all into account in every new scope document would be tough but I was determined not to miss the tiniest bit of detail again. Although the approach helped, details were naturally still missed and mistakes kept being made.

Conclusion

If you have a fixed, small project, Waterfall can be a good way to get it built, especially when outsourcing. But in software development, there are few fixed projects. Even when you think you have a fixed project, if it's successful, you'll want to build on it and if it fails, you'll want to fix it.

Waterfall can leave you with a product nobody wants that has been poorly designed and coded. It's like building a city where you're not allowed to change any plans once you've started building. It may be months before a critical flaw becomes apparent and by that time, it's too late.

It is a testament to the team I was working with at the time that even with Waterfall, we were still able to produce good work but the system we were using was not just holding us back but positively injuring us.

Luckily, we learned from our mistakes and moved onto a

more flexible system...

9

Transitioning to Continuous Development

Agile software development is about software development becoming more reactive to business needs.

The best-laid plans of mice and men often go awry but despite this, many tech teams plan months in advance of a project getting underway under Waterfall. When something inevitably does go awry, time and money get wasted.

The agile solution is to make it easier to release code more often, divide tasks into more bite-sized chunks and make it possible to change plans quickly. This is especially important in startups.

My first experience with Agile

We had a new custom-made website and could develop it how we liked. We were able to make a fresh start and take a different approach. The development team and product managers came together for daily stand-ups (mini-meetings where dev teams outline sprint progress and where they may need help or clarification). Product managers and developers started working together one-on-one. Projects were cut down into more bite-sized chunks.

When the new CTO came in, he advanced ideas started by our first CTO – ideas which seemed dangerous to those of us who had not seen them work in practice. These included giving developers business goals rather than solely technical ones; in small autonomous teams serving a product area rather than having one team serving every business requirement.

We started moving towards 'continuous deployment', in which you deploy code to the live environment frequently. This seemed dangerous because whenever we deployed, it took hours and something often went wrong. After deployment, the new code would be buggy and we all had to work overtime to make it work again, which meant another risky deployment. We tried not to release more often than once every two weeks.

Resistance

As the management team pushed the new policies, there was resistance from the dev team.

I remember multiple times sitting in the pub with developers who voiced their concerns. How can you make autonomous teams around different product areas when all teams share one code base, they asked. What happens when one developer from one team deploys code to the shared code base and the other teams don't know about it? What happens if a team deploys their own code and soon after it conflicts with another team's code? There were many practical problems to solve.

As for this idea of continuous deployment, it was unworkable. One of the developers had spent months improving the release process and it still took hours to complete. Other than that, our code base was unstable and it was written by one dev who had left the business and the others didn't understand it. We had too many problems to work through before we could deploy once a week, let alone several times a day!

Development slows down

Despite the concerns, we pushed on. Things started slowing down. There were miscommunications and people didn't understand how this was going to work.

About a month after we started making major changes, I was in a meeting with the CTO and the founder to discuss why the development process was slowing down. Looking back, as people get out of their old habits and try to learn new ones, it is always going to be a difficult time. It was a challenge for the web development team but despite their reservations, they wanted to make it work.

Autonomous teams were created. After months of toil, the

devs managed to reduce deployment time to five minutes. We started deploying more frequently and things went wrong. Different product teams produced conflicting code and sometimes someone would release code to live (production) that another other team had written but not finished testing.

A culture change

Soon though, things did get better. I stopped writing long scope docs. Instead, I planned my sprints with my team. Problems with the tasks in the sprint were picked up in sprint planning, rather than much later when development was already underway.

A single feature would be split out into several Jira tasks and each task would have its own mini-scope.[1] These tasks could then be done by anyone in the team at any point during the sprint. Splitting up these projects into multiple tasks meant that it was easier to test and code them. The scope for each task was clearer and more likely to include every necessary detail.

The product team I worked in sat together in own own area and I was available to my developers in case they needed something clarifying. Scopes could be changed even after they the developer had started work on the tasks. The increased collaboration meant features were released to real users much faster.

In my first four months, we worked in one and two week sprints. In the one week sprints, we would release at the end of the sprint. In the two week sprints, we would release once in the middle and once at the end of the sprint. As we were an autonomous team, it was up to us when we deployed and how we wanted to work. This in itself was a completely new experience for some of the developers.

Moving to fully continuous deployment

In the next few months, continuous development became possible. We had worked hard to get our systems ready for it, with tests written at every level and an improved deployment process. But I was apprehensive. Even releasing once a week could cause problems so to do it the moment a task was finished felt like a leap into the dark.

Despite my doubts, we found that the smaller the releases, the more stable they were. Bugs were found quickly. We did a release once every other day.

Not only did continuous deployment make releases more stable, it also meant that we could experiment with features faster to find the right answers for the business.

Every step a startup makes is a step into the unknown - a hope that this is where our customers want us to be. In these conditions, the more agile you are, the easier your business can find the answers that will make it grow.

10

How to Say No (or Sometimes Yes!)

One of the main parts of a product manager's life is to prioritise competing priorities in your backlog. Not just potential features, but bug fixes and sometimes even Ops tasks. In your roadmap, you will have a guide for what you are going to do in each week of your quarter. Everything feels very neat. You have a plan; it's a plan that your stakeholders have agreed to. What could possibly go wrong?

Well, a business never grows to a plan, definitely not your plan, and external factors affect the business to which it must react. This means that your stakeholders' priorities will sometimes change and it means that other departments will need things from you along the way. Often, these other departments won't understand your plan or what other priorities there are. They feel their need is urgent and often you may hear something like "But it's only a button!" or something similar. Can it not, *should* it not just be added quickly to your current or next sprint?

Debates without data are wasteful. They can continue for hours and neither side can prove the other wrong. Luckily, in a lot of cases, all meeting members will have the same business goals, and if they want to disrupt the agreed upon roadmap, they need to provide evidence that the disruption will help reach those goals faster than what has been planned. They also need to prove that the urgency for this feature is greater than other tasks. A lot of disputes can be avoided this way.

As a product manager, if someone else can prove the business case for a particular feature, they have helped you, so you are happy to say yes! Even in cases where this department has a different set of business goals, they must still show the value of their request before you can discuss prioritisation.

Often you will hear something like "It will make our lives easier", "we've had a few customers ask for it already" or "I'm pretty sure it will make a big difference". Basing your backlog priorities on making a salesperson's life easier is no way to add value to the business, unless the business case can be proven.

Some of the features most commonly asked for are often the features which make the smallest difference. There was one customer problem I recently found a quick way to fix. It had been requested multiple times for months by lots of different salespeople. They were on the phone to customers who had been telling us of this problem. I had been on the phone to these customers myself several times. Customers were telling us they would downgrade if it wasn't fixed and it had been requested at least 30 times over several months. But funnily enough, during these months, no customer had downgraded because of it and few had mentioned it among the secondary reasons they downgraded.

Eventually, I found a quick fix for it and prioritised it. After the fix, there was little return for the business. It moved us no closer to our business goals; it didn't slow down customer attrition. Was it worth it? It may have been, but it's hard to prove. It's a good example of how pressure can build up from both customers and salespeople for a solution to a problem that isn't making a big difference to people's behaviour.

Twitter widgets here and little contact forms there, task and feature requests will come at you every day. To stem this tide, communication is key. Have a roadmap that points to the themes you will be working on at different points of the quarter without going into any detail. This will give colleagues the context they need to understand if their product request can fit into your plan. Being clear about your team's targets with colleagues will make saying no easier if their request is left-of-field or will make saying yes a joy if their request will help you on your way.

A	B	C	D	E	F
Quarter target: 30% of new registrants order groceries twice within their first month					
	Week 1	Week 2	Week 3	Week 4	Week 5
Registration					
Upgrade					
Grocery ordering					
Weekly planning					

If you have a strategy and a goal, you can't do something else unless there's a good reason. The invisible cost of doing 'something else' is normally much greater than the value gained from building the feature. In a startup environment, where you always have only so much runway in front of you, saying yes to most requests is the road to ruin. Laser focus on that one goal you have set yourself is needed if you are to reach it.

11

Stakeholder Management

Getting your stakeholder management right is vital for you. Poor management can lead to drastic changes of direction and micromanagement mid-sprint. This kind of ad-hoc management will lead to confusion across the business and waste valuable dev resources. But stakeholders can add a lot of value to your team if you get the relationship right.

The first thing to note is that each stakeholder is different and you will have to adapt to their style. Some will get stuck into the detail and come up with grand new plans after a few minutes of discussion. Some can be very laissez-faire and others will be so busy that they can only send 5% of their concentration your way.

In reality, the best way to deal with all these different types of stakeholder is the same.

Before you start the quarter, you should have done the research to prioritise themes for the upcoming quarter. Product strategy research takes at least a month to do, especially because it's just one of the things you have to do each day.

After research, you are ready to take your plan to your stakeholder. You should be prepared several weeks before the start of the next quarter. If you want to have the greatest influence on product strategy, come with a solid plan to your first quarterly strategy meeting. This is for two reasons:

- Your plan will be the starting point of the quarterly strategy. The final plan will probably look something like your original one.
- Your analysis is likely more in-depth than that of your stakeholder's. It's your product area, and your stakeholder can't spend nearly as much time researching and analysing as you can. He has to trust you.

Weekly stakeholder meetings

You should always remain apprised of the business goals and direction, which is where your stakeholder can be most helpful. They will be in meetings you may not be where decisions are made that affect your product. You should have weekly meetings with your primary stakeholder where you update him on progress, agree on the next sprint (if you work in sprints– my preferred method is Kanban inside a sprint – see the glossary at the end of the book) and be briefed by your stakeholder on recent upper management meetings and the state of the business. These meetings should last no longer than 20 minutes because most of the communication you have with your stakeholder should have happened when you agreed a roadmap or continuously outside these meetings.

Communicating with your stakeholder

Your stakeholder is a busy man (or woman), so make life simple for him. A stakeholder wants a high-level understanding of how the PM's product area is performing. Are you on schedule compared to the roadmap? How close are you to reaching your business goals set at the start of the quarter? Giving stakeholders this information regularly means your meeting will be shorter and they will trust you more.

For the best communication, you should have a progress report on the themes in your roadmap. Below is a table showing how your product is progressing from a software development point of view against the goals of the quarter.

Journey	Goal	Completion Risk
	Main quarterly goal: 30% of new registrants order groceries twice within their first month	
Registration	70% completion rate	
Grocery ordering	80% completion rate	
Recipe filing	50% save 1 recipe from their first week	
Weekly log ins	3 on average	

Goal Completion Risk	
Green	Low risk, on schedule
Yellow	Some risks and/or behind schedule
Red	We won't reach goal under current circumstances

You should also have your product research in a spreadsheet for your quarter's work. Your roadmap, progress report and research report should all be separate sheets in the same spreadsheet – preferably a Google Sheet. The benefit of Google Sheets is that sheet updates are instantaneous so your stakeholder can always be up to date. The benefit of everything in one place is that communication will be much easier. No more fishing around for the right spreadsheet among the hundreds of others.

Auto reporting

Automate reports on your main metrics to keep everyone on the same page.

I put my three most important metrics, as well as my cohort graph in an email to my primary stakeholder, the Head of Product and all members of my team once a week automatically. This approach may need a data engineer, but it it's worth looking at because it can save you time, keep your entire team focused and your stakeholder up to date.

Different stakeholder personalities

As mentioned above, there are different stakeholder personalities but if the structure and plan comes from you, all of these types of stakeholder can be treated in a similar way. You should be aware that the more hands-on stakeholder may have ideas or ways of working that you will need to integrate into your plan. The laissez-faire stakeholder gives you a lot of freedom but therefore a lot of responsibility. If you don't come up with the specific business goals, it might be that no-one will; if you don't schedule the weekly meeting and make sure it happens, it may just not happen. The stakeholder who's spinning ten plates at the same time is in a similar boat. You will need to be structured with your communication with him. Make sure that you have their undivided attention for some time of the week; write emails with 'Please reply' if you need a reply quickly; make sure you stay in the picture with them.

Conclusion

Stay on the front foot. The more you can do this, the more likely your product development will be stable and the more your stakeholders will trust you. Constant and sometimes automated communication makes stakeholder management easy.

12

How to Deal with Bugs

Bugs are the mud beneath your feet. You can see your goal –
it's not far away – and you're running towards it but then, out
of nowhere, this puddle of mud appears and you fall flat on
your face. You get up and start running again before another
patch appears and you fall again. Learning to deal with bugs
so you can reach your goal in good time is vital.

Have a staging/QA site

This is a bit of a given but in everything I write below, I am
assuming you have a QA/staging site which the developers
release code to before releasing from their local environments
to live (production). If you don't have a site like this, you are
playing with fire every day because bugs in code are inevitable.

Prevention not cure

You need to prevent bugs from happening in the first place. There is a system of testing at every level before a feature is released that needs to be part of the coding process. It is a three-part process.

1. Test-driven development (TDD) means you write your tests before you write your code. These tests show you where your code is failing before you make more mistakes.
2. A system of integration tests, which tests that individual bits of code (units) work coherently together.
3. Automated regression tests check that the core functionality of the site still works, regardless of whether or not it has been changed in your latest release. A lot of bugs have a knock-on effect on something else and you sometimes can't predict what they may affect. You will want to check all your core functionality before every release. Sometimes, you will want to do some additional manual testing on your QA/staging site before release to make absolutely sure.

A note on manual regression testing

At small startups, there may not be automated regression testing. There may be no unit tests either and the dev team may not know TDD. In all these cases, you may be the only barrier stopping bugs reaching your users. It may be up to you to do all the regression testing manually. I would recommend that you encourage other members of the team to do this testing with you – partly because it's their job as much as yours and partly because it will give them the motivation to automate the process.

As your product grows in size, automating testing becomes more important. But even when you do a really good job of testing, you are still going to get bugs in your live (production) environment.

How to scale your product in a stable way

The more your product grows, the more you have to maintain: APIs, micro-services, hard-coded logic – it could be anything. There is a lot you can't control. Maybe you only recently joined a team which already has a large badly-written code base. But once you are in the team, as the product manager you are always responsible for your product area. If you don't get the product under control, you'll always be spinning plates and one will eventually break.

- **Alerts:** so the first thing you need to get set up is a system of alerts on your major systems. Do you rely on a micro-service? You and your team should get an alert the moment it goes down. You probably have a system of payments and billing set up – have you made sure it's still processing payments? You may end up with a major problem if there's no way of knowing the moment it fails. In the past, I've used a Geckoboard screen which the whole team could see so we could see the systems' status in real time. I also suggest an email or even text message alert – especially if something happens at a weekend or out of hours, for example.

- **Visibility:** you will also want to make sure that with everything you build, it's easy to figure out where the problem is. I've heard a number of times from developers something like "We have no logs of activity or errors on that particular system, so we can't figure out where the problem is". Making sure that they have visibility on any bugs or problems is their responsibility and to the benefit of the devs, but it's worth showing that you care about this too.

- **Documentation:** important system information should be documented in a wiki. If there's no documentation and your team of developers changes, your new developers may have no idea where to start. I've even had occasions where the dev didn't know how to access the system, let alone find and fix the problem inside it.

The point with alerts, visibility and so forth is that you can't have a huge code base and multiple micro-services in your product area without a way to easily and automatically maintain them. Otherwise you will always be stuck in the mud.

There will always be pressure from business to get things done faster. Many non-technical people in the business side won't understand or appreciate the need for improved visibility, alerts or auto-testing. They just want a feature live and once the code has been written, then it's ready, as far as they are concerned. You need to show your dev team that you believe in quality and finishing things off properly because you are the link between business and tech. If you don't show business that these things need to be done, some devs will do what the business wants. You may get away with this a few times, but if you keep doing this, you are building a house of cards.

The Five Whys

In Eric Ries' book *The Lean Startup*, he mentions the 'Five Whys', which is an incredibly simple concept. It just means continuing to ask why until you get to the root of the problem.

I was once working on a project when suddenly our system sent a batch of users an email they weren't supposed to get. I stopped the dev doing what he was doing and asked him to find out immediately what had happened. After he had found the immediate cause, I got the entire team into a room to discuss what went wrong.

The immediate cause was simple: the dev had made a mistake. But why had none of our systems picked it up? Because we hadn't got time-based testing set up. Why had we not got time-based testing set up? It was too complex and we never had the time. And why had the dev made the mistake? Because our database system was too complex. Why was our database system too complex?

You get the point. In most cases, people may just think "Oh, the dev made a mistake, mystery solved", and they hope it doesn't happen again. In these cases, you fix the immediate bug but you don't discover the problems with your system. But with the Five Whys, the can of worms below your bug start to appear. You need to fix these systematic failures if you are going to successfully scale.

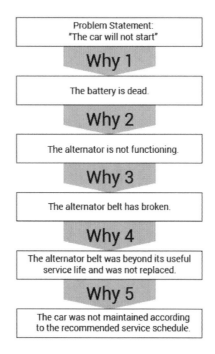

Example from Genroe.com

Reporting bugs

You also need a system where people from around the business as well as your users are able to report a bug. Initially, I did this by email. People would email me and I would look into the problem. You can probably see immediately the flaws with this system. Emails get lost; no-one else other than the reporter can see there's an issue; no-one can see progress on fixing the bug.

After a while of this, I set up a Trello board and I invited everyone in the business to join. Here are the columns I added:

- Bugs – where a bug could be reported

- Ideas – anyone can offer an idea to my product team
- Fixing – see which bugs we've prioritised to fix
- Fixed in Live
- Not a bug – after investigation, not a bug (but may still be a UX problem)
- Won't fix for now – let the team know what we can't prioritise right now

Trello is great for this kind of team collaboration. Here's why:

- Everyone can see everyone else's bug.
- Everyone can see how each bug was progressing.
- Everyone can see any comment that I make on each bug so they can see technical details and the outcome of our investigation.
- It is easy for me or the devs to investigate a specific problem.
- You can @ anyone in the team and they get an email notification.
- You can add screenshots of the bug easily.
- You can easily add the Trello card to your Jira task (if you use Jira).
- You can have one place to communicate with the entire team. I can get ideas from across the business and everyone can report problems easily.

You will want to set up a new board once your current board gets overfilled with cards. I did this once every two months, but it'll be different for every team.

Avoid major rebuilding or refactoring projects

Sometimes, the devs you work with will give you a doomsday scenario. Everything's going to fail unless we build everything from scratch again. So far, my experience is that things aren't like that and when a big refactoring project is undertaken, it can also go wrong.

Refactoring means improving the code. Developers take pride in their code and some developers actively want to make their code beautiful, which is great! Sometimes they don't want to work with other people's code and they often refer to 'legacy code' which means old code which has been written in an outdated way or a way which doesn't work with modern frameworks so well. Sometimes it's just their language for someone else's code written a while ago which they don't like.

Refactoring is good in little bits and pieces but more dangerous if undertaken as project. In product development, we are changing many parts of the product all the time. Refactoring code you will soon change anyway is an inefficient use of time and may cause problems later if it has been restructured heavily. For this reason, it's better to refactor and improve quality as you develop rather than stop development to refactor.

All other options should be considered first before a big refactoring project takes place. If a refactoring project is being considered to improve page speed, for example, there are other questions you can ask first. Do you really need those high-quality images and features on that page? What's the cost of the (estimated) salary and time of the dev team working on this project compared to the cost of taking out elements/reorganising the page?

When to prioritise bugs

Some people condone stopping development every time there's a bug. I've experimented with a concept called 'Bug duty' where one dev is always on duty to investigate bug reports (after I've done some basic vetting to confirm it does really look like a bug).

When to prioritise bugs depends on the number you get in on a regular basis. Ideally, any bug found should be fixed immediately. If you get a lot of bugs, you need to prioritise carefully. You have business goals to reach. You can't get too distracted. In these cases, you may want to get the most important bugs fixed, reach your goal and then come back for the others. I've done this a few times and it's worked well.

If you've set up the structure with testing, alerts, visibility, the five whys and so forth that I've set out above, this shouldn't happen and if you enter a team where it is happening, you need to express the importance of dealing with it to your business stakeholder otherwise it will forever be eating at you. No-one wants to deal with bugs, least of all your dev team, who are there to build great new products, like you!

Avoid QA or bug investigation teams

QA (quality assurance) teams are great for devs; devs can get on with coding and someone else can ensure the quality is there. But, of course, the quality of the code should always be the responsibility of the coder. If someone else has to write the tests and ensure the code can get released, the coder won't have the incentive to write the highest quality code. The consequences of their sloppily written code won't come back to them. Any role the QA team might play should be filled by you and your team.

Conclusion

Dealing with bugs is simple. Prevent them from happening first (tests, tests everywhere!). Know the moment something goes wrong (alerts and easy bug reporting). Make it easy to fix (visibility and documentation). Do a post-mortem whenever something does go wrong (the five whys). Improve code quality every time you touch an area of your code (mini refactoring).

13

Feature Bloat: Why Features Sometimes Aren't the Answer

One of the things you will always be tempted to do is add another feature. It is, after all, called product *development*. But with every new feature comes a lifetime of maintenance; another plate to spin in the air.

Take a look at WhatsApp and you can see that they've kept it simple. There must have been pressure on the business to build video calls, for example, early in their development. Instead, they've kept their app simple. They've been able to scale because they focused on the fundamentals. As more users signed up for their service, they were able to keep a high quality service serving their most fundamental needs. There are nearly always ways to optimise the core service your website or app offers, and nearly always backend work that needs to be done to improve structure and stability. WhatsApp have implemented end-to-end encryption, for example.

The result of this focus is a genuinely lean business. Despite having hundreds of millions of users, in 2014, the business only had 50 employees.[1]

"WhatsApp's extremely high user engagement and rapid growth are driven by the simple, powerful and instantaneous messaging capabilities we provide." Jan Koum, WhatsApp co-founder and CEO

Another example is Google. While Google have now branched out into pretty much anything they feel like these days, in the first 5 years of hyper-growth, their focus was entirely on making a simple tool and make it the best it can be.

What you want to avoid is the idea that if your product performance is faltering, you need a shiny new feature to add to it and prop it up. Especially if you haven't made serious attempts at optimising the product, you can't be thinking about making add-ons. You need to focus on making your core product work. Of course, if you've optimised to your best ability and the product is still faltering, it might be time to pivot to a different business model. But the pivot can't come before the optimisation process. If it does, you have potentially wasted your time building your initial core product without learning its potential.

The other problem with adding new features is the maintenance cost. Every new feature you add is a new lifetime cost to the business and a cost/benefit analysis of the feature must include the lifetime maintenance cost of that feature. One of the things I have learnt is that there is little more wasteful in a tech company than wasting a web developer's time building something you don't need (excluding hackathons and certain forms of experimentations).

14

Time Management

You are responsible for the strategy, research, design and detailed specification of your product. On a daily basis, you need to coordinate with multiple departments and respond to new business needs. This is especially true if you work in a startup, where there may be no design team or no SEO team, for example; it will be up to you to make the decisions on particular details. Time management is vital to be effective.

Automate as much as you can

In previous chapters, I've written about how I automate tasks to make my job easier. Here are processes I described:

- **Auto alerts:** at VouchedFor, I set up automatic alerts the moment one of our major systems failed, like our connection to Intercom, for example. This meant we knew the moment there was a problem and didn't have to go looking for one when a salesperson came to us with a bug report.

- **Auto reporting:** I set up an automated email with our progress on our quarterly metrics. I got it sent to the team I worked with as well as my primary stakeholder, so we could all know how we were doing. Every meeting with my stakeholder could start with relevant information already known.

- **Auto testing:** extensive automated testing at every release, so you don't have to do much manual regression testing. It is also more reliable than your manual testing and means you won't face time-consuming bugs in the future.

Internal communication through transparency

Having interruptions is an inevitable part of a product manager's day. I found a major reason I was interrupted was when someone didn't know when they were going to get something from my team. Sometimes we had released something that someone didn't know about or didn't understand how to us it. Occasionally, people didn't know what had happened to a bug report someone else had sent me and when it would be fixed.

All these interruptions can be solved with clear, transparent communication. People need to know what your team does, what its strategy is, how it is implementing its strategy and when bugs will be fixed.

Product vision and yearly strategy: people should know

what your product vision is. If people know what you are trying to achieve, they can offer more relevant suggestions and questions. They may filter out suggestions they know you won't do or realise that they should be directed at a different product team. Similarly, letting everyone know the major themes you plan to tackle in the coming year will provide greater context for who you are and what questions should be directed at you.

Roadmap: a clear, simple roadmap which shows which themes you are going to tackle this quarter in which week will make it clear to everyone when they can expect something they need.

Weekly product show and tell: each week at VouchedFor, the product managers would stand up in front of the entire company and list the big things we released in the past week and what we plan to release in the coming week. We would also demonstrate some of the features we had released on a big screen. There is an argument for doing this fortnightly if your product development is stable enough for that. At VouchedFor, there were between 40-50 people at the business during my last year there and we made the show and tell events optional. Almost everyone showed up most weeks and this was manageable. If you work at a big company, you will have to be more selective with invites!

Emails about releases: as well as the show and tells, I would send everyone at VouchedFor an email with what we had just released. Because we were releasing continuously, normally I would aggregate several releases into one email. Double communication means people are more likely to remember and for those not in the show and tells, it makes sure they also know what you are doing.

One Trello board for all bugs and ideas: everyone can see the progress, notes and communication on each bug report and can offer product ideas. This makes the bug process streamlined.

A clear quarterly progress report: as well as the automated metrics email, having a progress report with a traffic light warning system to show your stakeholder which themes or projects may not get fully addressed in the quarter means you can have streamlined meetings with your stakeholder. He doesn't need to ask about your progress because he knows about it already.

Plan as much in advance as possible

Two week sprints: having a two week sprint means you only have to do sprint planning and retrospectives with your team every two weeks rather than one. It means you have greater stability to your product development which means you can plan more in bulk in advance.

Bulk Jira ticket writing and backlog grooming: pick a day of the week that makes sense for your product cycle, go somewhere quiet, put in your earphones and write up all the Jira tickets not just for your next sprint, but ones which you are confident you will do soon. Make sure you add this to your company calendar, so people don't try to set up meetings with you then. Get everything done:

- acceptance criteria
- description
- wireframes with notes
- epics where several tasks are part of the same theme/feature
- backlog grooming to get rid of tasks you won't do
- backlog and sprint prioritisation

Another major source of interruptions is your dev team asking questions about how something should work. This not only interrupts your flow, but theirs too. Ideally, your dev team should be able to develop without you – everything should be prepared for them. Of course, in an agile environment, we know there are unexpected issues, but where things can be made clear, they should be. It also means that anyone can see the spec of a task if they need to look historically.

If you have all your wireframes and scopes ready in advance, you have plenty of time to get sign off from your stakeholder if you need it.

Visibility

One thing that may waste your time and that of your dev team is when the cause of a bug or problem isn't immediately obvious. Part of this is getting to know your product well technically with all of its quirks. The other part is ensuring that all your systems have as much visibility as possible to identify a bug quickly.

At VouchedFor, we used a tool called Raygun, which tracked all the errors users faced.[1] Sometimes, the error reports logged in Raygun were useful and sometimes they were not because the error description didn't provide much detail. Optimising these processes will save everyone a lot of time – you if you are the one investigating the bug and salespeople if they are trying to figure out what the customer they're speaking to is seeing.

Using queuing systems like Gearman can provide the extra information you need to see where something is. In fact, the more we logged in a clear and structured way, the easier it was to find the source of the problem. If you don't log actions your site takes automatically or those based on user action, it's time to start.

Data analysis shortcuts

If you are not careful, you may spend hours on a specific piece of data analysis. SQL can be fiddly sometimes, especially if you are working with a large database. Other sources of data can also be fiddly. But luckily there are shortcuts.

SQL: keep a 'Useful SQL' doc and add to it whenever you have written some SQL that will be useful in the future.

Google Analytics: save segments and then once you've built a report, you can save the report as a shortcut, so you can always come back to it.

Intercom: in Intercom too, you can tag certain users or save segments of users

Customer service email analysis: I have used HelpScout in the past which certainly does well for the problem it's trying to solve. Later, I moved our customer service to our integrated Intercom solution. In both, you can tag conversations and get a list of these conversations later, so qualitative analysis via these tags is easy. Since it will be your customer service team who does the tagging and not you, make sure to keep your list of tags clear and simple – they have their own job to do too.

Timeboxing – keeping you focused

Nothing should take more of your time than its worth. It doesn't matter whether it's data analysis, a meeting or a bug investigation, sometimes a task needs to be timeboxed. Not only does it focus the mind, it also makes sure you stay effective in your job. If you find you are working until 8 each evening, it probably means you are not being effective with the hours in your day.

My team and I agreed to timebox our sprint planning and retrospective meetings to great effect. Before, we would go down a technical tangent which could last for half an hour. After timeboxing, we would finish in double the time. We would do the planning and retrospective together and combined, it would take us sometimes as little as 40 minutes when we timeboxed it – that was with two week sprints to plan and with five members in the team too. It's worth doing – your combined salaries amount to something when you're all in a meeting together.

The biggest danger to a product manager

The biggest danger to a product panager from a time perspective is that all the urgent stuff gets done first, leaving no time for the important stuff. Dealing with bugs, coordinating with other departments, being in meetings, making small but necessary decisions on the detail of a task or feature – these things come first. And in a startup, sometimes there can be a sudden change of direction from management based on a marketing experiment elsewhere in the business.

So the important stuff – speaking to customers, analysing data, thinking through and writing up Jira tasks properly – doesn't get done. The product manager must be laser-focused on his or her quarterly goal. You need to leave time for the important stuff each week, even when the urgent stuff seems overwhelming.

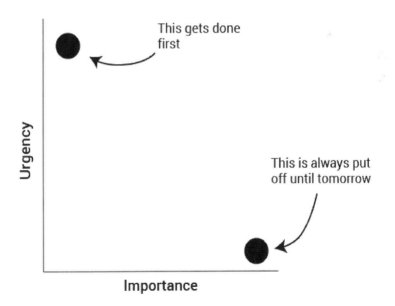

15

Sprint Planning and Retrospectives

Since sprints would start immediately after the last one ended, we found it made sense to do a retrospective and planning meeting at the same time as we transitioned from one sprint to the next.

What is a retrospective?

As the name suggests, in a retrospective, we would look back at the last sprint and figure out what we did well and what we can improve.

Is it worth doing?

Some PMs don't and sometimes in a continuous environment like Kanban (see glossary) it can be difficult to arrange but I think it is worth it. Agreeing ways to work more effectively is worth it. Being open with each other about what went wrong and what went right is helpful.

It certainly isn't worth doing every week because not enough happens in the space of a week, but since we did two week sprints, doing one at the end of every sprint made sense.

How do you conduct one?

In a lean startup, there shouldn't be too many people in your team so it should be possible for everyone's suggestions to be heard.

The important thing is that everyone feels comfortable to say what they really feel.

The way the product teams I have been involved with decided to do it was with post-it notes. One member of the team would hand post-it notes to the other members and they would write down all the positives from the past week. Each member would then read out his positives. Getting people to write down their thoughts before discussing it meant that team members weren't influenced by each other and everyone had to contribute. After everyone read out their points, I would tally up the most common points and we'd have a short discussion about them if there was value in it.

After the discussion, we would repeat the process with things we can do better. Then we would agree actions for the next sprint so we can work more effectively. For example, there may be an agreement on a new way to accept pull requests (a request by a developer to release some code to the next environment) so work can be released more quickly; or it could be about the number of meetings the team is in and how to lower that number because it's getting in the way of the coding flow.

I would then write up the discussion on Confluence, part of the Atlassian suite that also contains Jira. I did this so we would have a record of the actions we agreed to take and would remember to take the actions after the meeting was over.

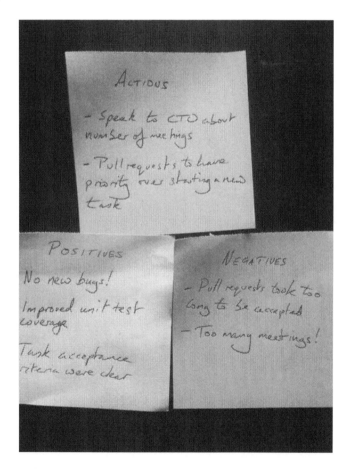

Sprint planning – how to keep it short and sweet

Before each sprint, you need to estimate each task in the sprint so you know which tasks you can leave in and what to take out. Here's how to do it in the most efficient way possible:

1. **Specify:** think through and fill out the detail of the Jira tasks in full at least a day before sprint planning
2. **Estimate alone:** estimate the size of the tasks yourself. I estimated by number of working days for a single developer, since the sprint is also measured in days but some PMs prefer estimating in other ways.
3. **Estimate with an expert:** there may be a development manager of the tech team you can go through the sprint with or do it with a member of your team, skimming through each task, to get a more educated guess of the estimates of each task. Doing this with a member of your team means the sprint planning meeting can go faster because one member of the team has thought about the task from a technical point of view already.
4. **Estimate with the team:** in the sprint planning meeting, describe the task in question and ask each member to write down the number of days they think the task will take. We went down to 0.25 of a day but no lower. Again, some teams prefer t-shirt sizes (i.e. S, M, L as the size of a task), but my preference is number of days. Once you've estimated all the tasks for the next sprint, the meeting is over.
5. **Add extra detail:** add any extra detail the team pointed out. Sometimes a Jira task needs to be split into multiple more bitesized tasks.

6. **Deprioritise:** probably some tasks will have to be taken out of the sprint based on the estimates of your team. In your sprint planning you did separately and earlier with your stakeholder, the priority of tasks should already be clear, so you don't need sign off on the deprioritisation, but send him or her an email anyway with the official sprint.

Sprint plans are flexible. Sometimes something not in the sprint needs to be done or a piece of analysis shows that one task is a higher priority than another one. In Agile development, it's ok when priorities change mid-sprint.

As mentioned in the chapter on time management, we time-boxed our sprint retrospectives and planning meetings in teams I worked in. With five members of the team and a two-week sprint ahead of us, we managed to keep these meetings to only 40 minutes.

16

Your Product Roadmap

Once you've got a product strategy signed off, you can move onto your product roadmap. This is a roadmap of the themes you will tackle within a certain period.

It is *not* a detailed plan of all the features you will release in that time period.

To have that detailed plan would be to presume that each feature improves your product and once done, you need to release the next for further improvement.

The reality is that you never know the effect of a feature or a design improvement until it has been user tested. You will start off with a hypothesis like:

People aren't using FoodZube enough because the meal planning side has missing something. If we add side dish recipes to the weekly planner, we will see greater user engagement.

That's fine as a hypothesis but then you need to test that hypothesis rigorously with data you already have and by speaking with users and potential users. And to make sure you keep moving forward, this research should be done continuously.

In these agile circumstances, adding 'side dish recipes' to a roadmap would be a mistake. The feature you end up building several months down the line may be very different to the one you currently have in mind.

Roadmaps I've created sometimes look as simple as this:

	A	B	C	D	E	F
Quarter target: 30% of new registrants order groceries twice within their first month						
		Week 1	Week 2	Week 3	Week 4	Week 5
Registration						
Upgrade						
Grocery ordering						
Weekly planning						

This shows what journey the team is focusing on and when. Anyone in the business can look at this roadmap and know what we are doing – indeed, more detail may make it more complicated for people outside the team to understand.

If you have a bigger team and a bigger, more complex product, a roadmap as simple as this may be over-simplifying. Gov.uk's roadmap doesn't go by week but does let you know what's just been released, what's in progress and what's coming up.[1]

Even then, gov.uk doesn't go into detail about a feature, often using a phrase like 'design away' or 'iterate'.

Gov.uk have also made their roadmap publicly available. In

principle, any way you can get your user base more engaged is good – being transparent is a great way to do this.

Your roadmap itself can be a place to get user feedback easily, especially if you use Trello. Users can comment and vote easily on ideas in the roadmap.

There are legitimate worries about opening yourself up to competitors with a public roadmap but with Trello, you can set permissions to view and even just invite certain customers if you want. Within the business, at least, being transparent with your roadmap will improve communication with colleagues.

Conclusion

Roadmaps are about communication. More detail doesn't mean better communication. Make sure to say what themes you are focusing on, but provide too much detail and you may cause your own problems when a colleague says "But you said you were going to do this" when the likelihood of you doing what they thought you were going to do was actually pretty low.

Share your roadmap with everyone in the business – show them the value your team brings and the plan you have.

17

How to Prioritise Product Development

Prioritising your backlog of tasks is one of the core parts of a product manager's life. Product development is about progress and learning; if you get the prioritisation wrong, you miss a key insight. Get it right and your business can get ahead of the competition.

The size of your business matters

In a small startup, generally the founder takes the 'product manager' role or there may be just one product manager. In this scenario, you don't need a formal process to manage multiple priorities because you likely don't have them. You likely only have the money for a small dev team and can only focus on one thing at a time.

This can be a great moment because it forces you to stay focused. Develop your core product until it becomes clear you have to pivot, or just keep going.

In a large business, there are a lot of business goals and a lot of research is often done up front. As per *Lean Startup* principles, even big companies can be lean and an iterative approach is still helpful.

I learned how the process of product prioritisation evolved as VouchedFor grew from a team of six to a team of fifty. Here are some of the lessons I learned.

The basics of product prioritisation

Product prioritisation can be boiled down to two quite simple and obvious factors: time and impact.

How long will it take to complete a project/task?

What will the project/task's impact be?

You want your task to be little time, high impact but how do you calculate effort and impact?

In terms of time, I have always done it by number of days for a single developer, which has turned out to be the best form of estimation of those I've tried.

Impact is based on your business goal (OKR/KPI). If your goal for the quarter is to increase your sales conversion rate on your e-commerce site to 10%, adding a new section on the

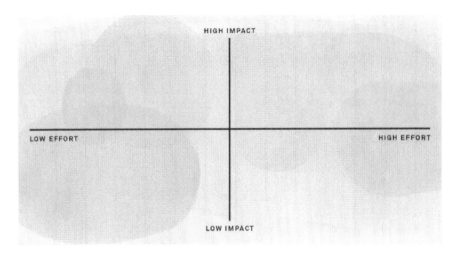

HIGH IMPACT

LOW EFFORT

HIGH EFFORT

LOW IMPACT

Via Intercom

site for TVs is not going to help reach that goal, even if the new section would have an impact on margin and revenue. It's impact is, therefore, zero.

I normally judge impact on a scale of one to ten, but there's no reason why that is best particularly.

Before my meeting with my primary stakeholder, I list out all the tasks up for contention for space in the next sprint in a spreadsheet. Included is my time estimate for each task, which I do in conjunction with a developer on my team. My stakeholder and I then go through the tasks and assign an estimated impact of each one. Our highest priorities then become clear.

Using this process has made a big difference to both the speed and effectiveness of my weekly stakeholder meetings.

Before, the stakeholder meeting would be largely based on gut-feel. Impact and time would be a big part of the discussion but not in any structured way. Meetings would go on for

Task	Time	Impact	Impact/Time	Priority
Task A	3	6	2	4
Task B	2	5	2.5	2
Task C	1	7	7	1
Task D	4	9	2.25	3

too long as we debated priority without any framework to base a decision on.

We do occasionally disagree with priorities based on the numbers of course, but it gives us a good guide and challenges some of our biases for or against a particular task.

Your quarterly business goals

It is ideal to have a one main goal for the quarter. All your efforts for the quarter lead to that goal.

I've been in situations where my product area has had multiple goals and you have to weigh up the impact of different goals as well as the impact of a task or project on reaching a goal. This makes prioritisation one layer more difficult, as well as making the quarter lose focus.

Estimating the size of a sprint

The starting point for estimating the size of a sprint is the number of developers and number of working days in a sprint. However, this will give you an unrealistic view of how much you can get done. If you are working with a new team, I suggest taking 10% of the days calculated off the sprint.

If you've already experienced a few sprints with your team, you can judge velocity based on your previous sprints.

In Jira, you can see your sprint velocity for previous sprints in a bar chart. It is based on the number of 'days' (i.e. points) you actually got done. You will be able to estimate quite accurately the number of 'days' your team will do in the sprint.

Add your taxes

There are three taxes I normally add to my sprints: ops, bugs and small tasks. These are things either out of your control (like ops sometimes is), things you don't know will come up (like urgent bugs) or things which have to get done fast (like a change to the Ts & Cs). The extent to which you need any of these taxes depends on the product and company you are in.

If it turns out that you didn't need all the time set aside for these types of tasks, your team can simply move onto the next task in the backlog.

Taxes added, you've now got a good idea of what you can get done in your sprint.

No snacking

"It's just adding a button!"

There's always something small that someone wants done. But they should be prioritised along with everything else.[1] Every '30 minute' task still requires a code review and breaks up the focus of a dev during the day. The real cost of a '30 minute' task is much higher, and if you are prioritising it just because 'people want it done and it won't take much time', you won't know if it has a good chance of making an impact.

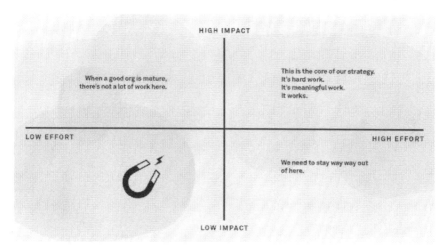

Via Intercom

Do projects/epics in one go

Teams I have been involved with have nearly always done their best work when everyone was working on the same project, we knew what we needed to do and how long we had to finish the project.

Doing an entire project in one go also means that the whole team is involved with development strategy and a more holistic view is taken. This means that when the teams are changed, some members of your team will still be familiar with a major part of your product. It also means the quality of the whole project is likely to be higher.

When measuring time and impact, it's worth taking entire projects into account.

18

Working with a Remote Dev Team

There are advantages and disadvantages to devs working remotely. I remember one specific day when a dev was working from home for just that day and he managed to get four separate major tasks completed, ready for code review the next day. One of them was annual pricing!

Working remotely lets a dev focus – one of the most important things a dev needs. Without focus, code quality decreases and tasks take double the time. When working in the office, interruptions are guaranteed. Someone needs their code reviewed, someone has a question about how something works, meetings happen. So remote working has its advantages.

Why work in the same place

However, working physically together with devs as a team

brings a team spirit. At one stage, a team I was in had its own official name, together with team t-shirts (bought with our own money) and traditions, all of which we had fostered within the space of three months. By the end of this period, we knew each other well and the devs knew each other's code well. There's nothing quite like pair programming or going through a code review together for a dev to get to know their colleagues and how they like to write code.

Equally, devs were able to show me a section of code they had written and take me through it so I would know the code was written based on the logic I had specified. We were able to spot several misunderstandings before they got any further.

And designing your app sitting with your dev can save a lot of time.

I remember one time we were working to such a tight schedule that there was no time for a proper prototyping or UI design phase. Wireframes went straight into the page's front-end code. The dev and I sat together and got the task done, making sure the design was right as he was coding it. At the end, we had created a very successful design for our MVP and we had done it in record time. This wouldn't have been possible with a remote dev, or without the team spirit we had picked up.

How to work well with a remote dev team

Scope: The key to working with a remote team is to make your task scope thorough and accurate. This is a good exercise anyway and working with a remote team can keep you disciplined. As outlined in the chapter on time management, you should write out all your acceptance criteria and include all wireframes, screenshots, prototypes etc in your Jira task. By doing this, your team can work without your direct involvement for several days.

Without a thorough scope, some remote teams will feel it's on them to fill in the gaps and 'just get it done' for the client. You may end up with the wrong thing and a remote team which guesses the answers.

Recognise their work: in a lot of cases, I have seen a remote developer go the extra mile for his client, working very late hours for sometimes weeks in a row without significant recognition. Sometimes it's hard to realise the work someone is putting in half way around the world when it's still 4pm local time for us, but 10pm for them.

I have found that recognising both the work and dedication of a remote dev can lead to a beneficial working relationship. They are more likely to go the extra mile for you. And I have found that giving remote devs a feeling of ownership of the project, even if they're not an employee, can help build a team spirit even when they're thousands of miles away. Sharing with them the result of their hard work – e.g. 500 new customers were able to access this new way to sign up to our app since we released your work yesterday – makes them feel valued.

The result from a team spirit point of view is that I have been invited to the homes of people I've never met in person before. The result of greater spirit is greater dedication to the company and to the app we're developing.

Conclusion

I have worked with several remote teams and several in-house teams. While working in-house is preferable, remote teams can be almost as good. As long as you pick the right team and get your side right on the scope and recognition, your remote devs will work well without your supervision.

I would also suggest that in-house teams offer their devs one day a week to work from home to guarantee at least one day of singular focus.

PART FOUR: TOOLS

19

Google Analytics: The Basics

Google Analytics is a free but in-depth tool to figure how your site is performing. Upon first use, Google Analytics can seem confusing but you can quickly pick it up. It's important to use it in a smart way because otherwise you can spend hours on it, reading vaguely interesting stats without providing you with the real insight you need.

In this chapter, I will explain some of the core features you will need and how to hack GA so you get the information you need with minimal effort.

Let's start with the first screen you see and the menu options you have

Audience

In this section, you can find out what type of people your

users are. Are they male or female mostly? Do they use a mobile, tablet or desktop mostly? How old are they?

When you click on this tab and explore a little, you will find all this information easily.

Acquisition

This section tells you where your customers are coming from. Which channel e.g. organic? Social? Referral? Direct?

The section can connect to your AdWords account to see what behaviour customers from your PPC campaigns are showing and can also connect to your Google Search Console account to give you data on which of your site's pages people are landing on and where your pages are ranked in Google.

Behaviour

This is where you can find out what people are doing on your site. Are they visiting a page and immediately leaving? How long do they spend on an individual page? Which are your most popular pages?

This area has a lot of in-depth data. You can see the most popular user journeys people undertake, you can see people's behaviour based on their landing page and check which pages need to load faster.

Data on events and what people are searching for are also there.

There's also Experiments, where you can set up A/B tests and In-Page Analytics, where you can see where people are clicking on the page. Instead of Experiments, I would suggest using a tool like Optimizely.[1] For In-Page Analytics, a tool like CrazyEgg is more appropriate. These features tend to be quite buggy – I've rarely got either to work well.

Conversions

The Conversions section lets you easily find out how well your site is performing on-page. Are people signing up for your newsletter? Are they registering?

Once you've got goals set up, the Conversions section becomes very useful. I used it most frequently for the registration journey. How many people were dropping out on the landing page? What about step one of registration and what about step two?

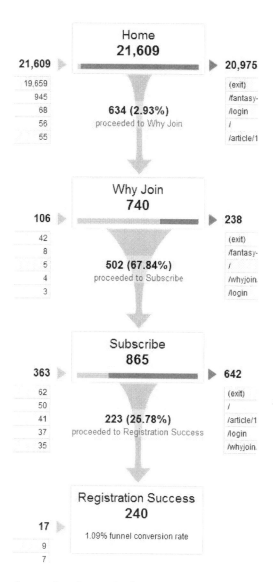

You can see from the funnel above how helpful this is at pinpointing problem areas of important user journeys.

Setting up goals

One of the first things you should do when you set up Google Analytics is define your goals. Here's how:

Step 1: Go to Admin

Step 2: Click on 'Goals' and add a new goal

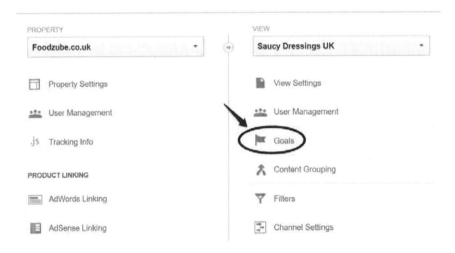

Step 3: Choose 'Custom' unless one of the default options make sense for your goal.

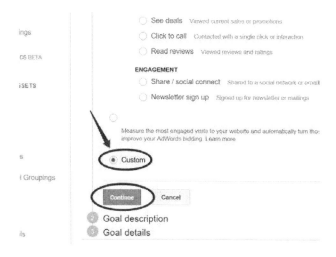

Step 4: You can choose different types of goals. Destination and Event are the most common types – one of these is probably what you want. A destination is a page. An event is when a user does something like clicked play on a video or pressed a button, for example. You have to set up events manually.

Step 5: Provide the details of the goal. Enter the destination page if you are using that type of goal. This step is where you can add a funnel and a value for a complete goal.

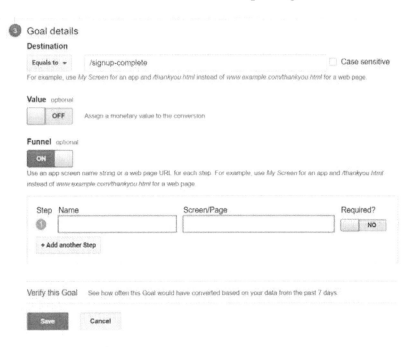

You can only set up 20 goals, so make sure to focus on the most important ones. This is actually a good feature because it can stop you getting swamped in a sea of data. There's always the temptation to dig further and see things from more perspectives, but that will ultimately be counter-productive.

Setting up events

Events are incredibly important to understand your site's performance. Google can't know what a particular button or video means for your site unless you tell it. If you have a page which tries to convince visitors to sign up, and you have different sections on it, videos, accordions and so forth, you will want to have events on all of these.

You will want to answer questions like 'Does the video on the page improve conversion?', 'Do people look at the pricing section'? and 'If I look at these stats by device, how useful are these elements of the page then?'.

To set up an event, you need to add a snippet of Javascript to the button or action you want to track.[2]

For every event, you can describe it in three ways, two of which are mandatory.

Category: a way to group events e.g. Registration page

Action: what the event actually is e.g. 'click' or 'play'

Label (optional): a description of the event e.g. 'Top Sign Up button clicked'

You can find yourself with dozens of events so getting these three descriptions right is important when you or a colleague is trying to find information quickly.

Setting up segments

To draw insight out of your data, you'll need segments. This is another way of tracking goals too, especially when the number of main site goals are limited.

At VouchedFor, for example, I set up segments to track sign-ups by type i.e. financial adviser, accountant or solicitor.

Once you've set up a segment, it's saved in your Analytics

account to reuse.

You can add a new segment on almost any report you are looking at regardless of which section you are on but you should be aware that any segment you make while looking at that report will be created in relation to that page. For example, I added the segment 'Direct Traffic' to a report on one content page:

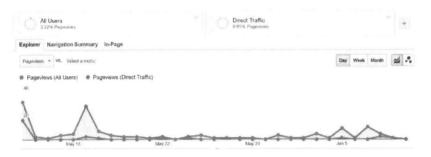

The Direct Traffic segment only refers to this page, as you can see.

To set up a new segment, simply click on '+ Add Segment':

You can then choose from a pre-made segment from Google or set up your own. To set up your own, press the '+ Add Segment' button here:

You can either choose a simple segment or set up a custom one based on custom conditions or custom sequences. If you choose a sequence, it means your segment of users will all have followed a particular journey through your site.

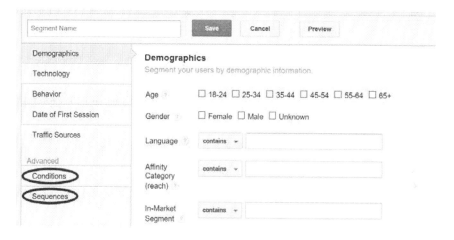

Once you are done, press 'Save'. You can add as many segments to a report as you like.

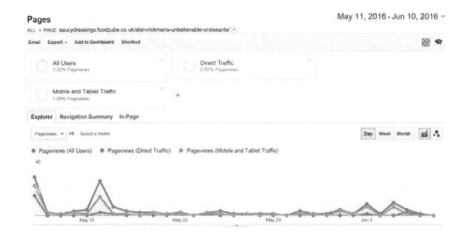

Avoid a Segments mistake I made

When I set up a segment which included an event, I did it on the report for the relevant page. So at VouchedFor, for example, if I wanted to find out how many professionals had invited a client to leave a review, I went to the report for the 'Invite Clients' page.

As I created a new segment, I went to the 'Conditions' tab and added the Event Label filter. The event was pressing the button to send a message to the client.

Once I saved the segment and went back to the report, I thought it would show me the number of times that event was triggered. I looked at the pageviews column for insight.

However, when I went to the Event tab in the 'Behavior' section, looking specifically for that event to check the report was telling me the right thing, it gave me a completely different statistic.

The lesson is that if you are making segments with events,

you need to make your segment in the event report, not the page report.

Shortcuts

You may want to save some of these reports with your custom segments. This is very useful and incredibly easy. You do it by making a shortcut:

You can then find all your shortcuts easily.

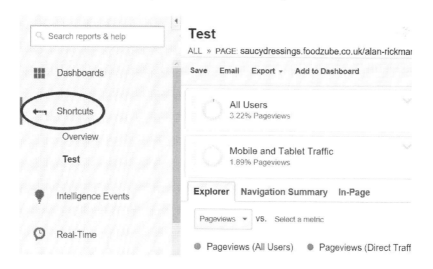

Interpreting the data

Google Analytics gives you the raw data. How you interpret it is what makes a good product manager.

Compare historical data: you can compare your current performance with previous performance. Make sure to always compare equal sized time periods.

Here's how you do that:

So you can see immediately how you're progressing. In the example above, more work is needed on getting people exploring more of the site, getting the bounce rate down and increasing the average session duration, but some great improvements have been made in terms of number of visitors.

Here are some tips when comparing historical data:

- When comparing an old period of time with the past month (or whichever dates I was using), I would always compare a few periods rather than just one. You can never know when a data point could just be an anomaly.
- You can compare historical data on any report.

Comparing historical data

- Make sure you have a large enough sample that your data is statistically significant.
- Your site changes over time. Are you sure you're comparing apples with apples? If it's not clear in a project management system like Jira when a new feature went live or something significant changed, you may want to make a note of these changes somewhere like a spreadsheet so you don't end up comparing incomparable data.

Interpreting the bounce rate: you can expect different types of pages to have different bounce rates. Sometimes a high bounce rate can be good. The bounce rate is just when some-one visits your website and leaves the site without visiting any further pages.

If the goal for your page is to download a guide, for example, and the goal can be completed on that page, a high bounce rate coupled with a high guide download rate suggests the site visitor found what they wanted from your site immediately and the page is successful.

Most of the time, though, a high bounce rate is bad and you will want to lower it as much as possible. You will want to compare yourself to similar sites to know if your bounce rate is at a healthy level and how much more you can realistically expect to lower it.

Interpreting average time on page: this can be a bit mis-leading. Google Analytics measures time on page only when the user moves onto another page on your site. So if your bounce rate is 100%, GA will tell you the average time on your page is 00:00:00. Take this stat with a pinch of salt. Again, a high average time on page may mean that your visi-tors aren't finding what they need quickly. If you have a high average time on page for one of your important pages, you will want to look at what people are doing on that page with CrazyEgg and Inspectlet.

Performance by source: you'll find that your site's perform-ance can vary drastically by traffic source. People visiting your site via Google will have different expectations and are visiting your site with much less time on their hands than someone who comes direct. A visitor from a social network may give your site more time if a friend has recommended it.

Compare your source traffic to historical data to see how you're being found and how different types of people behave on your site.

Take all data with a pinch of salt: an early employee of Google once told me if people knew of the bugs in the Google Analytics software, they wouldn't trust it as solidly as many do. Google Analytics can have difficulty understanding the traffic data from your site, especially if your site uses the Angular framework. Sometimes, you may have misunderstood a metric in a report or you may have set up your segments wrong. It's always worth sense checking data from GA. You can do this with:

- Other data from GA
- Data from your database
- Data from Intercom
- Any other data sources you may have

Secondary dimensions: you can look at the same data in two ways on Google Analytics. For example, if you want to see users not just by browser, but also by screen size, you can add a secondary dimension.

You can see conversion by screen resolution and browser, for example. This can be useful for picking up bugs on a particular device and browser. There are lots of ways and reasons to use a secondary dimension.

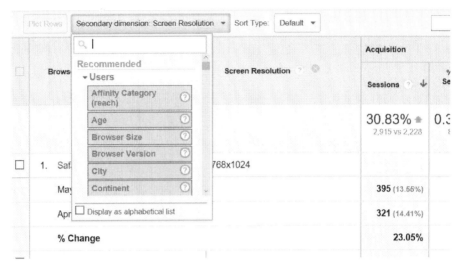

Browser	Screen Resolution	Acquisition			Behavior
		Sessions ↓	% New Sessions	New Users	Bounce Rate
		2,915 % of Total: 100.00% (2,915)	88.47% Avg for View: 88.47% (0.00%)	2,579 % of Total: 100.00% (2,579)	87.89% Avg for View: 87.89% (0.00%)
1. Safari	768x1024	395 (13.55%)	84.30%	333 (12.91%)	86.84%
2. Chrome	360x640	385 (13.21%)	88.05%	339 (13.14%)	87.01%
3. Safari	375x667	300 (10.29%)	87.67%	263 (10.20%)	92.33%
4. Safari	320x568	284 (9.74%)	85.21%	242 (9.38%)	90.85%
5. Chrome	1366x768	180 (6.17%)	96.11%	173 (6.71%)	87.22%
6. Chrome	1920x1080	123 (4.22%)	76.42%	94 (3.64%)	73.98%
7. Chrome	1280x800	59 (2.02%)	93.22%	55 (2.13%)	84.75%
8. Safari	414x736	53 (1.82%)	92.45%	49 (1.90%)	92.45%
9. Firefox	1366x768	47 (1.61%)	89.36%	42 (1.63%)	97.87%
10. Chrome	1280x1024	43 (1.48%)	97.67%	42 (1.63%)	97.67%

Conclusion

I found that the further I dug, the more features it turned out Google Analytics had. The guide above provides an introduction, but there are add-ons and many features not covered here. There is, for example, a whole section in GA specifically for e-commerce sites. A lot of your decisions on A/B testing, for example, can come from Google Analytics data, but you can also investigate bugs and find out more about your audience from it.

20

Intercom: Your Secret Weapon

Research in product management can be a messy, long-winded business. And knowing the right time to contact your customers can be a guessing game. Intercom changes all that. You can research user segment needs easily, reach out to users at the right time and get feedback quickly.

See who your customers are and how they are responding to your product

There is a free version of Intercom available which is easy to install. If you're on WordPress, there's a plugin. If not, there's just a bit of Javascript code to add (you'll end up with quite a few bits of Javascript to add for different products – this is where a product like Google Tag Manager or Qubit can make things easy).

Once installed, you can see when and how your customers use your product and who they are. You can see how many users haven't logged in within the last 30 days, for example. You can find this out with the 'Last Seen' filter:

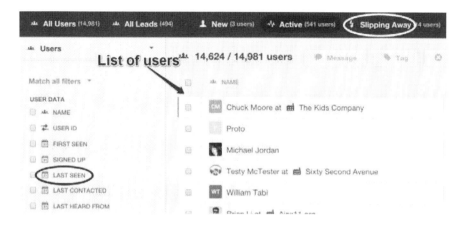

You can also use 'Slipping Away', which a pre-made segment which does this for you. But as you can see from the screenshot, there are many ways to filter your users e.g. you can see what proportion of new users are logging in multiple times in their first month at both an individual and company level.

In-depth user insight

Like with Google Analytics, sending custom data to Intercom gives you insights tailored to your app. In Intercom, there are two types of custom data you can provide: events and attributes.

Events are things that your customers do in your app, like press a button.

Attributes are things that describe your customer, like

whether they are an accountant or financial adviser, in VouchedFor's case.

Going back to the example of the food planning and delivery app FoodZube, let's look at what attributes and events it may want to use.

Here are some examples of what FoodZube would want to know about its users:

- Paying subscriber status
- Food blogger status (has the user started a FoodZube food blog?)
- Signed up with Facebook?

Here are some examples of what FoodZube would want to know about what its users *do*:

- Added a recipe to their recipe collection from Food-Zube
    o How many?
    o When?
- Invited a friend to send them a recipe
    o How many recipes?
    o How many friends?
    o When?
- Got their weekly shopping delivered
    o How many times?
    o When?

With the help of a developer, you can send all this information to Intercom. After some time, you can see a rich history of what every individual user is doing on your site.

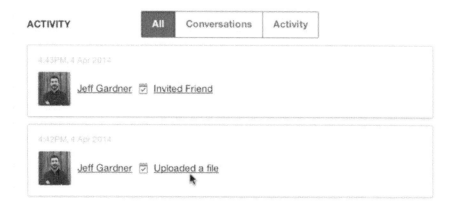

You can do this on a macro level too, finding out what proportion of your users got their shopping delivered in a particular week.

And you can go into detail. For example, you can track which users visited the grocery delivery page and left it before completion. You therefore know which users to contact to find out why they left.

Targeted, automated messages

Now that you have all this information on who is doing what and when, Intercom moves beyond mere analytics. What first drew me to Intercom was the ability to send targeted messages to our customers in an automated way. I knew that if VouchedFor was to scale, we needed a way to keep customer service quality high in a more automated way.

For FoodZube, for example, you could send out a targeted message to users who had got their shopping delivered two weeks in a row but hadn't done so for the third week.

When you send out a targeted message like this, you can add

a goal. In the FoodZube example, the goal might be to persuade the user to get their groceries delivered again.

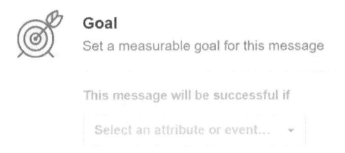

And you can see the performance of a message clearly, with sent, open, click and goal rates all clear.

To be sure you've optimised your message, you can A/B test them if you have a large enough user base:

A downside to automated messages is that you may annoy your customer with too many messages when they don't want one.

For that reason, Intercom has a filter called 'Last contacted', which means if the user has recently been contacted, you won't send them this auto message.

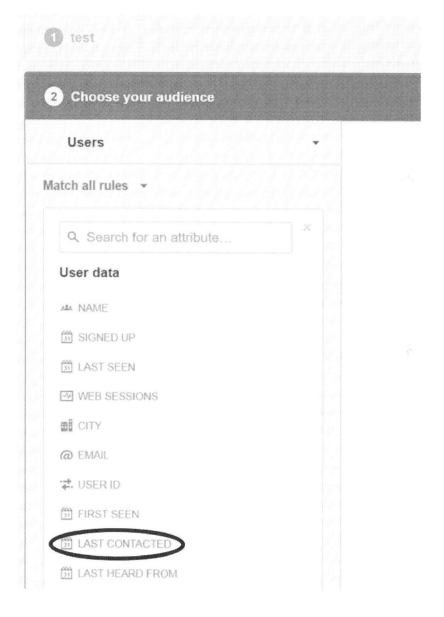

And to avoid contacting users at the wrong time, you can also set up a delivery window:

You can communicate with your users in three ways:

- in-app
- email
- push notification if you have a mobile app

At VouchedFor, our customers didn't need to log in every day, so we often found email to be the best form of communication. For other products, a push notification or in-app message may be best. Sometimes you may want to send a push notification to your customer to notify them that they have an in-app message.

Ideally, you would send a message to users at every step of their journey with your product, from registration to optimised usage. If your messages are successful, this can free up your account management team to focus on more advanced support for your customers.

Learning from targeted messages

Before Intercom, VouchedFor used HelpScout for our customer service email. In order to gain insight from customer communications, I asked the account management team to tag conversations based on a list of tags I had provided. These tags were things like 'Upgrade', 'Inviting Clients' (to get reviews) and 'Pricing'. I found the tags were often unhelpful – either they were too broad, in which case I couldn't find meaningful feedback or they were too distinct, in which case the sheer number of tags caused confusion among the account management team.

When we started sending targeted messages from Intercom, however, I found I was able to gain feedback easily. We sent messages to users at every step of their journey, so it was easy to see user feedback for that step and how engaged users were at every step.

If someone wasn't getting reviews, we could find out why. If someone didn't finish registration, it was easy to find out who and why. If someone quit while in the process of upgrading, we could find out why, in the context of who they are and their previous activity on the site.

Sometimes, you may want to send an automated message not to get a user to take an action, but simply to get feedback. Something like

"We see you've bought your weekly shopping for an entire month with FoodZube! Congratulations! We were wondering how your experience was? Is there something we could improve?"

You can get simple feedback with emoticons or in-depth feedback with full replies.

The learning you can gain from your customers using Intercom is several levels above what was previously possible.

A single way to communicate

Before Intercom, at VouchedFor we used HelpScout, Gmail, Dotmailer, MailChimp, Mandrill, Olark and the phone to communicate with our customers. Sales used HelpScout, Gmail and Olark. Marketing used Dotmailer, Gmail and MailChimp. Product used Mandrill.

None of us knew what communication the others were sending or at what time. As VouchedFor grew fast, sometimes it felt like there was no time during the day to coordinate to the level we needed to. We had up to 15 account managers and salespeople manually communicating by email or phone with our customers. We sent out automated messages every day and there were marketing emails which went to certain batches of people sometimes several times a week.

We had both an overload of communication and often conflicting communication going out to our customers. When I did focus groups with everyone involved with our B2B customers at VouchedFor, one of the themes that came up again and again was this lack of a singular communications strategy which got everyone on the same page.

In my product strategy presentation to the Head of Product and CEO at VouchedFor, I included this diagram:

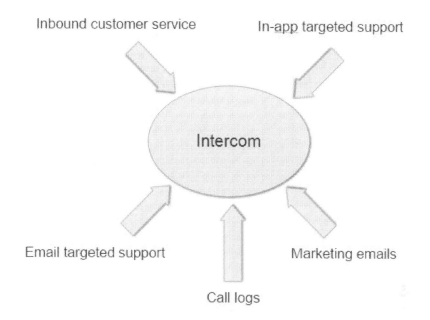

Intercom was able to replace nearly all of the different communications systems we were using and improve upon them at the same time.

As well as automated messages, Intercom was able to send manual targeted messages (replacing MailChimp), be our customer service email (replacing HelpScout) and host our help docs (again, replacing HelpScout). The automated messages largely replaced Mandrill and the live chat feature replaced Olark.

We were also able to send customer call logs from our CRM to Intercom.

Now we can see a full history of all communications between a particular customer and ourselves, whether it was live chat, via phone or via auto or manual message. We also know when the last time was we contacted them so not to overload them.

Perhaps most importantly, everyone in the business can see our communications strategy. They can see what messages we're sending out, what channel we're using and when they'll be sent. There's no confusion when a customer rings up and asks about a particular message they received from us. This transparency can help move the company to the next level.

Top tips with Intercom

Intercom has been great for us but there are some things it doesn't yet do well.

CRM: At first, I thought Intercom could replace our CRM. It has a lot of the features of a CRM but crucially, it's missing call logging.

Historical data: Intercom gives you the current state of play, but you can't compare two time periods, for example, or look at your data on a graph. You can send data from Intercom to a 3rd party app, which can do this for you.

I've also had significant difficulty ensuring Intercom gets a constant stream of accurate data. Since Intercom and everything you do on it runs on data and you rely on its accuracy, you will need to get this right.

On one of my projects which used Intercom, we set up a queuing and logging system so you could see exactly what data was being sent and when. If data stopped being sent to Intercom, the team was alerted immediately.

Originally, we used Segment to connect our site to Intercom but we lost visibility of the flow of data by doing this, so we reverted to a direct connection.[1]

Conclusion

Intercom can help with your product research, automate your customer service and unite everyone under one communications strategy. You can enable or disable any message at any time, A/B test all messages, reach users through multiple channels and make it easy for users to reach you. You can help users at every stage of the sales funnel and build deeper relationships with them. Whether you are building a web or mobile app, Intercom can probably help you.

PART FIVE: SKILLS

21

SEO: An Introduction

Some product managers won't need to know about Search Engine Optimisation in their jobs but in most jobs, you will come across it at some point. When I entered product management, I presumed that since SEO was a technical subject, the developers you work with will know it. Mostly, my experience is that they don't. Sometimes a dev will ask you how to design your company's permalink (URL) structure. There may be a question about breadcrumbs or sitemaps. You will want to know the answer not just so you can make the right decisions but so you can see your product in the context of how it gets discovered. It may open up new ideas for growing your business.

What is it?

In simple terms, SEO is about how to be found on Google. You may want to give some thought to Bing and some SEOs include other search tools like YouTube, but I'm going to stick to Google here.

Why Google?

Google's US market share is around 64%. Its nearest competitor, Bing, took around 20%. In other markets around the world, this can change dramatically in Google's favour. In the UK, 87% of the search market was cornered by Google, for example. Quite simply, Google dominates.

First steps

You need to set up Google Analytics and Google Search Console as your first priority. If your business email is run with Gmail, this will be easy, but anyone can sign up for a Google account, even if you don't have a Gmail email.

Once you are set up with an account, you will need to add some Javascript code into your site on every page you want to track. This often means you can add it to your website HTML header or if you are using a WordPress site, you can use a plugin like the one from MonsterInsights that will make your life easier.[1] You can find your tracking ID and the code you need in Google Analytics at Admin > Property > Your site > Property Settings > Tracking Info

Here's the page for a site I own:

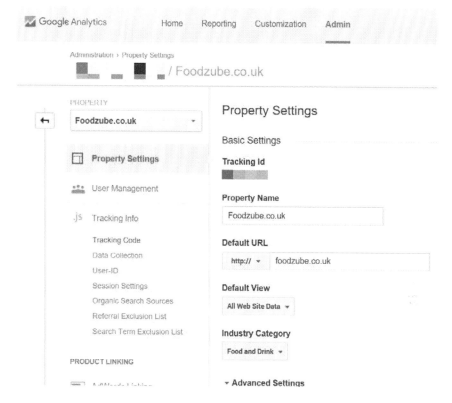

Next, you will want to set up your Google Search Console, add your site and verify you own it, which you can do using your Google Analytics account.

There may be a few other tools you'd like to set up. Here are two I would recommend:

- **Moz Toolbar:** gives you insight into how sites from across the internet fare with Google.
- **Yoast:** if you use WordPress, Yoast makes some of the technical SEO easy.

The parts of SEO

There are 3 parts of Search Engine Optimisation. There is technical, off-page and on-page SEO. Of the 3, I'd say off-page is the most important but each one is vital in its own way.

22

Technical SEO

Technical SEO means making your website work in a certain way that Google likes. There are certain things you need to do.

Sitemaps

Having a sitemap is necessary. Google will penalise you for not having one. There are two types of sitemap – XML and HTML. XML is the one Google reads and the HTML one is there to help your users find their way around your site. Google hasn't said so directly but Matt Cutts, the former head of the search algorithm, has hinted that Google looks favourably on sites which have an HTML sitemap. It's probably worth having because at the very least it will help a few users, even if Google doesn't give you a ranking boost.

As soon as you have generated your XML sitemap, add it to your Google Search Console (formerly known as Webmaster Tools). This means Google can easily crawl your site and it'll be indexed on the search results faster.

You can add as many sitemaps to Search Console that you like. Sometimes this may make sense, if you run a multisite, for example, or if you have multiple subdomains which are not directly related to your main site's purpose. The important thing for the sitemap is that your pages are organised neatly and simply.

Site structure

Your site structure is how the webpages in your site are structured. Do you use subdomains? If so, why? How many levels of subdirectory do you have? Why have you categorised webpage X under subdirectory Y? These are the issues you need to get right.

Each site will need a different structure but the most important thing is to keep things simple and easy to understand. A simple site structure will help both you and your site visitors understand how the site works and where to find things. A simple structure will also mean your site is easier to maintain.

As a matter of principle, you will want to avoid subdomains until further news comes from Google proving that they are safe to use. Matt Cutts spoke about the issue of subdomains vs subdirectories a few years ago, suggesting that Google doesn't mind which structure you use but Moz found evidence that subdomains can cause problems. In my experience, there have been some problems that we have theorised were due to our use of subdomains. Therefore, I suggest avoiding them unless it becomes clearer that they are safe.

Once you've got a site structure set up, it's important that you don't change it if possible. If you change your site structure, it means you are changing your URL structure. If you change your URL structure, site links which used to work won't anymore. Unless you do something about it, users from Google will get a 404 error (a 404 page can be an opportunity, by the way).

If you have to change your site structure, you need to set up a 301 redirect, so that when users or the Google bot land on your old page, they'll immediately be redirected to the new page. **Please note: you will lose a bit of your Google ranking score when you do a 301** and if you do more than one 301 redirect, Google gets more suspicious that yours is a spammy site. So avoid changing your site structure unless it is really necessary.

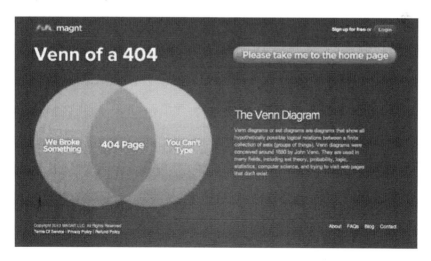

Make the 404 page interesting to turn it into an opportunity

Instructions for the Google Bot - Robots.txt

You can give Google instructions of what to crawl and what not to crawl in your robots.txt file. If you want a certain subdirectory not to be indexed on the Google search pages, you simply write:

Disallow: /subdirectory-name/

And you can add a * after or before the subdirectory to mean 'everything'. So

Disallow: /subdirectory-name/*

means that you want Google not to crawl anything which is in that webpage or any other webpages which are pages or subcategories within that subdirectory.

Some people also add their sitemaps to their robots.txt file to make sure Google can always find the sitemap and crawl your site easily. I think this is unnecessary since you've already told Google about your sitemap in your Search Console.

I recommend keeping your robots.txt file as clean as possible. The more you put in there, the more you have to maintain later. Someone will make a decision about your website 6 months later that affects one of the subdirectories you told Google not to index in your robots.txt file. Your site won't be doing as well as expected or a new webpage won't be getting any traffic at all and you'll be scratching your head wondering why. It's these types of problems that make product management difficult: you can't keep every technical detail in your head all the time for every decision. So really think what you *need* to disallow in your robots.txt file.

If you are running WordPress and you disallow your /plugins folder, it could mean that Google's bot can't render your page properly. The bot doesn't just read your page's HTML, it also looks at the CSS and Javascript, so blocking that folder may cause problems. The lesson here is to keep things simple because products are naturally complicated.

Noindex

Another way to stop Google indexing your page is to add the attribute 'noindex' to your page's source code. You should be aware that it is up to the Google bot to honour your request, which it nearly always does.

I strongly recommend you install something like the SeeRobots Chrome plugin so you can always check whether one of your pages is noindex easily.[2] The other way to check is to check the source code. To do this, right click, press 'View Page Source' and then press CTRL + F to do a search for the word 'noindex'.

You will rarely want to noindex a page. If a page is behind a login screen, there is no need to noindex it. If it's not and site users can see it, why don't you want them to see it via a Google search? If you are finding yourself using noindex on more than one or two exceptions, you need to question the approach you are taking.

Nofollow

The nofollow attribute tells Google not to take this link into account for its search algorithm. It doesn't mean that Google won't follow that link.

Nofollow is one to look out for. I have been involved in link-building projects where we pat each other on the back for getting a site to link back to us only to find later that they made all the links nofollow, so we won't get a benefit in the search rankings!

Often, I believe other sites add the nofollow attribute as company policy. I've known sites to nofollow useful links to other parts of their own site before, so I don't think there's always a conscious decision to nofollow. Often, all it takes is a quiet word with your contact at that site and they'll take off the nofollow.

It's worth noting that Google say they don't take nofollow attributes into account in their search algorithm, although it was a concept they introduced themselves in 2005.[3]

Breadcrumbs

Breadcrumbs are the map which shows you where you are in the site. They appear on most pages of a website and look like this:

Home > culinary serendipity > art, photography, sculpture

In the example above, it shows that this page is in the sub-category 'Art, photography, sculpture' in the category 'culinary serendipity'.

Breadcrumbs help users find their way around the site and Google likes them too for two reasons:

1. Their bots can crawl your site more easily because they can find the links and site structure.
2. They help users around your site, and anything that helps users Google approves of, in general.

It isn't proven that having breadcrumbs on your site gives you a rankings boost but it's definitely a good thing to have, even if it just reduces the bounce rate.

Occasionally, your breadcrumbs will show in the Google search results (SERPs) but there are indications that Google are phasing that out now. Here's what they look like when they do show:

HTTPS – make your site secure

There is some scepticism in the programmer community about how secure an SSL certificate really makes your site but Google certainly believes it's important.

The S of HTTPS stands for 'secure'. It means the communication between your web server and your browser is encrypted. To get HTTPS status, you need to buy an SSL certificate, which is often best to get from your web host. You can buy a standard SSL certificate or a wildcard SSL certificate, which is much more expensive. A wildcard certificate is only necessary if you have multiple subdomains you also want to cover, otherwise a standard one is fine.

Once you're set up, instead of

http://yoursite.com

it will become

https://yoursite.com

Having HTTPS gives you a small boost in the Google rankings. Beware though, it can slow down your site loading speed by a second or so.

Despite this, I recommend getting an SSL certificate for 3 reasons:

1. It does make your site a bit more secure. That's always good, regardless of if you are a bank or a personal blogger.
2. Google gives you a small rankings boost
3. You get this symbol next to your URL in your web browser:

This little padlock symbol is important to build trust with your site visitors. It builds your site's legitimacy and lets them know your site is secure. Not only is this a nice touch for UX, it'll also help lower your bounce rate, which will also help you in the Google rankings.

Site speed

Website loading time matters. As you can see from the graph below, every second it takes for your site to load, people abandon your site.

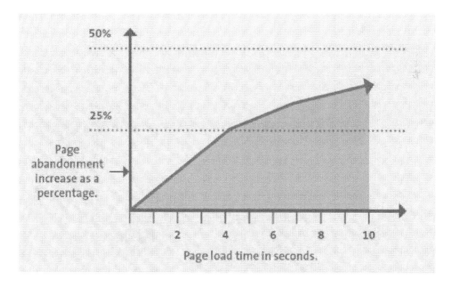

From QuickSprout.com

Google knows this too – ever noticed how Google is always the fastest website to load on the internet? It takes page load very seriously. You can measure page load speed in a number of ways, but I think it is likely that Google takes into account render speed – that means not just looking at when the HTML has loaded, but also the Javascript and CSS. I also think it likely that it looks at render speed for above-the-fold content especially seriously because of the suggestions Google provides on their PageSpeed tool.

You can use Google PageSpeed to improve your site speed. It provides you a speed score and suggestions for how to improve it.

You can see the score for one of my websites, foodzube.co.uk, here:

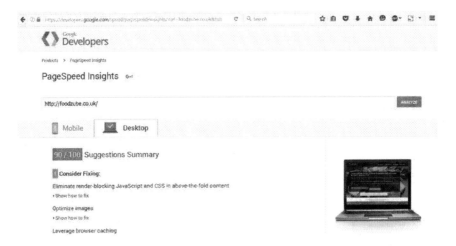

Ideally, your site should have a score in the nineties. On my WordPress sites, I have installed some plugins to solve some of the issues Google has highlighted.

- Imsanity – to stop me or any other site admin mistakenly uploading huge photos. Often, slow loading time is because your designer sent your developer a crazy large photo file, which the developer uploads and then the site is slow.
- WP Smush Pro – from WPMU Dev, this compresses your image size to optimise file size without losing photo quality
- Autoptimize – this eliminates a lot of the unnecessary render-blocking Javascript and CSS. It's a pretty awesome plugin – just beware that it sometimes has a problem with JQuery so if your site looks weird after you install this plugin, that's probably why.

Really, you should optimise all images and icons before you upload to your site, whether you use WordPress or not, but having something like Imsanity does stop you doing something stupid.

Caching

There is one way often used to reduce site speed: caching. Caching can be great; it means if your user has already loaded a page once, returning to that page can be near instantaneous. Using software like Varnish, if one person has recently loaded the site, all users after him will load the site a lot faster (until the cache resets).

This is great, but the problem comes when the user expects the content to change and it doesn't because the user is looking at a cached version of the page. For example, if you are making changes to your LinkedIn profile, press 'Save' and nothing changes, you presume there's something wrong with the site. You need to be careful with caching – it can be useful and in most cases should be used but make sure between you and your developer that you come up with a solution that works.

Accelerated Mobile Pages (AMP)

Website speed on mobile phones is a problem. On GPRS and 3G, page speed can be slow. Even on 4G, some pages can load slowly. Making your site as fast as possible on mobiles can be the difference between you and your competitors.

For this reason, a project supported by Google called Accelerated Mobile Pages makes a copy and restructures your page's code so it loads fast on mobiles. So you have two pages, one with a URL like:

Yoursite.com/your-page

And the AMP version simply looks like this:

Yoursite.com/your-page/amp

So your page will look pretty minimalistic. Here's a blog post from the blog SaucyDressings.com:

Original page	AMP version

Five Lemons, 2015: Copyright: Christophe Jonathan Clark Fine Art

QUICK CHRISTOPHER BRAMHAM INSPIRED TART

Quick Christopher Bramham Inspired Ler Tart

saucy dressings • 3 month

• art, photography, sculpture, ¡

• Christopher Bramham, Lemor

The result is that you can appear on Google's mobile results in an easily findable and nicely exhibited way:

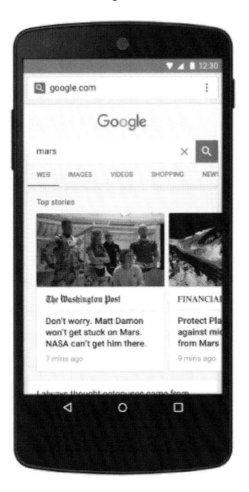

Duplicate content and canonical tags

One of the main ranking factors is duplicate content. If Google finds what it deems to be duplicate content on the Internet, it ranks one of the pages and the other one gets a huge penalty. Sometimes you will want to duplicate content, such as in the AMP case above. This is when canonical tags become useful.

Google will only accept one page if there's duplicate content, so the canonical tag lets Google know which page to rank and give all the Google juice to.

To add a canonical tag to your page, add the following line to the <head> of the HTML of your page:

```
<link rel="canonical" href="http://yoursite.com/page" />
```

Sometimes people wonder whether to use a 301 redirect, noindex or a canonical link. Here's a helpful table:

Instruction to Google	When to use
301 redirect	You've moved the page/got a better version
noindex	You have some duplicate content on a page that you are worried Google will penalise you for, but the page itself is unique. For example, I use noindex for blog category pages – it includes lots of duplicate content from the blog posts themselves
Canonical	When you need two versions of the same page, so you need to tell Google which one should be ranked in the SERPs

Duplicate content can spring up surprisingly easily. Google sees each URL as a different page. You've got to be really careful. At VouchedFor, we found that capital letters in URLs caused a problem.

So if we had a page like

vouchedfor.co.uk/bristol

and by mistake we also had a page called

vouchedfor.co.uk/Bristol

Google saw that as duplicate content.

In VouchedFor's case, as a directory with thousands of pages, URLs were automatically generated. You can't expect your tech team to know this kind of SEO, so you have to ensure that these things are thought about when building your site.

And just a small style tip – generally, avoid capital letters in URLs altogether. You will also want to check other seemingly inane details e.g. does www.yoursite.com redirect to yoursite.com? If not, it should, otherwise Google sees two separate home pages with duplicate content.

Luckily, you can use a few tools to check if you have a problem with duplicate content. Firstly, there is Google Search Console (Webmaster Tools). Go to Search Appearance > HTML Improvements to find where some of your duplicate content is.

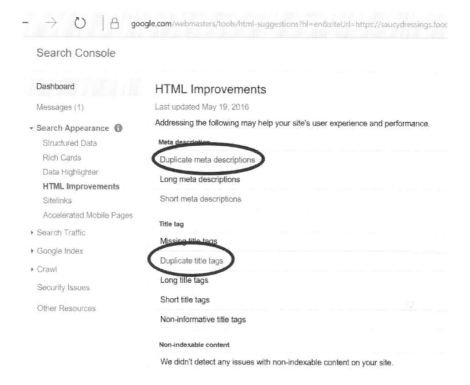

Two other useful tools

- **Copyscape:** checks the internet to see if anyone's duplicated your content
- **Siteliner**: checks for internal duplicate content

23

Off-Page SEO

Off-page SEO is your reputation on the internet. If you have a reputable website, other websites (preferably reputable themselves) will link to you. This has always been the basis of the Google search results. Today, Google's algorithm is complex and reportedly has over 200 factors but the links to your site are still important.[1] As a product manager, you won't need to know a lot about off-page SEO, as this is very much the realm of the marketing department, but you should have an appreciation of its importance.

Off-page SEO is about link-building. If you are getting a lot of links to a single page and you want to spread out the link juice, there is on-page SEO that you need to do. But off-page SEO is getting those links.

What type of links do I want?

You want links from relevant, high authority websites. It used to be that you could get links from anywhere. There were sites you could pay to give you a link, regardless of relevance, and link farms where people linked to each other just to get the link juice. No more can you do this and if you do, be prepared for a ranking penalty from Google.

One link from a high authority website is worth ten from low authority ones, so based on the 80/20 rule, I would focus on them.[2]

You can find out the authority level of any website easily with Moz's toolbar.[3]

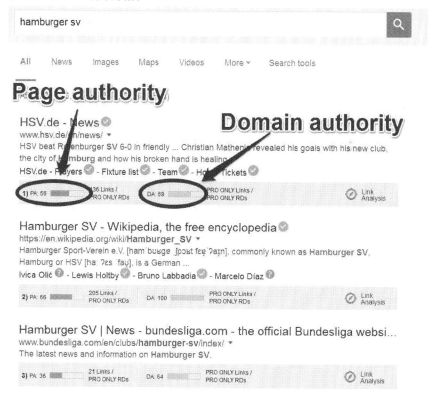

On the toolbar, 'domain authority' is the authority of the site and 'page authority' is the authority of the page. Domain authority is more important because the authority of a page is subject to change, whereas the authority of the site is less subject to change unless the site admins have been using black-hat SEO techniques.

Sites which link to you need to be relevant. If you are an e-commerce site for cake tins and you get a link from a renewable energy site, it looks suspicious. You should try to get links from sites which are genuinely related to the same topic as yours.

There are also generalised sites which can be great to get a link from. Getting a link from BBC.com is often seen as one of the ultimate ways to prove your reputation to Google, for example.

How do I get these websites to link to my site?

By adding value. Sometimes this can be easy. If you are an e-commerce site with a great deal on for an item lots of people want, other sites in your topic area may want to tell their users about it. But often, getting links from other websites is about writing great, in-depth content.

You need to contact the site you want to link to you and give them good reasons for them to do so.

Other than waiting to be found, there are a few common ways to get links to your site:

- **Guest blogging** – this is still good, despite Matt Cutts' warning.[4] Just make sure only to link to your site where it genuinely helps the reader, and be conservative about it.

- **Social media** – having a strong presence on social media and encouraging social media sharing will mean a greater likelihood of a site linking to you. You will also get a direct ranking boost in Bing.

- **Broken link building** – find links on a site you are targeting that don't work. Tell the site admin about it and let them know that you provide similar information/service.

You can find a great resource on link-building at Pat Flynn's Smart Passive income site.[5]

Widgets

Another way you can get links to your site is with widgets. TripAdvisor does this, for example.

You have to be really careful with this technique, however, as Google knows a lot of sites use widgets for SEO spam. Originally, Matt Cutts said that all widgets should include a nofollow tag but Google have since updated their recommendation.[6]

I reckon widgets can still be a good SEO technique if used with a lot of caution.

.gov and .edu links

Some companies go after .gov and .edu links as a matter of priority. I think this is a mistake because a) it's not been proven either way that these specific top level domains (TLDs) provide greater link juice than anything else b) they're not necessarily the most likely websites to link back to you, so you may be wasting your time compared to targeting more relevant websites.

24

On-Page SEO

Google ranks web pages based on what people search, trying to find the best matches for them. On-page SEO is about two things:

- Having the content that people are searching for
- Giving your site visitors a great user experience

You often have the content people are looking for but you have to show Google your content is the most relevant. Keywords are at the centre of this. You will need a good density of your target keyword(s) on your content and images without keyword stuffing; you may want to research keywords to decide what to write about or what to target; you will need to think about your meta description and your alt text on your images – these can include important keywords too.

As well as keywords, giving your site visitors a great experience is also key. It is just basic UX: putting yourself in your site visitors' shoes.

This is where your Google Analytics account will be vital. You need to know

- who your visitors are
- where they're coming from
- what they're looking for on your site
- where they are
- what device they're using

Each factor helps you model your site based on why your visitors are there and what they want. The more useful you can be to your visitors without trying to sell them something, the more they'll trust your site and want to return.

Finding the right keywords

Start your keyword research on Google AdWords' Keyword Planner tool. This tool provides statistics on monthly keyword searches and provides a list of keywords related to your topic you can target.

To keep things simple, let's say you want to write about lemon pie. You go to the Keyword Planner tool, type in 'lemon pie' and the category you are interested in. In this case it would be 'Recipes'.

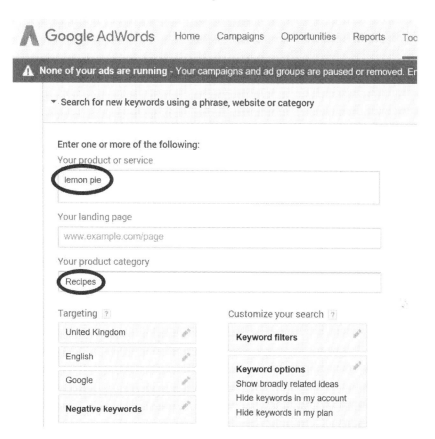

Click on the Keyword Ideas tab.

It looks like Lemon Meringue Pie is a popular choice. Let's see what the competition looks like.

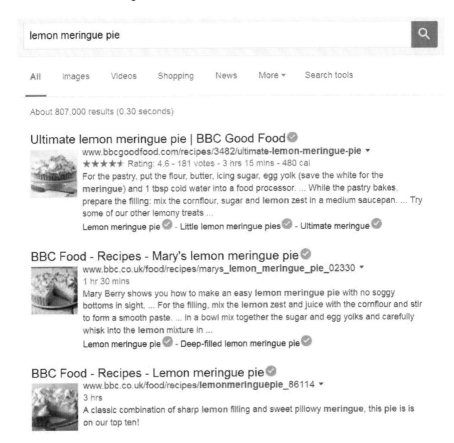

The BBC dominates. Below the BBC is celebrity chef Delia Smith's version. Below her, you have a *Daily Mail* version and one from All Recipes. You are not going to win here – these sites have premium domain authority. But scroll to the bottom of the page and you can see related searches that you might have a chance with.

Searches related to lemon meringue pie

easy lemon meringue pie   lemon meringue pie **gordon ramsay**

lemon meringue pie **biscuit base**   lemon meringue pie **condensed milk**

lemon meringue pie **jamie oliver**   lemon meringue pie **delia**

mary berry lemon meringue pie   meringue **recipe**

Still a lot of competition on 'lemon meringue pie biscuit base', so let's refine our search further.

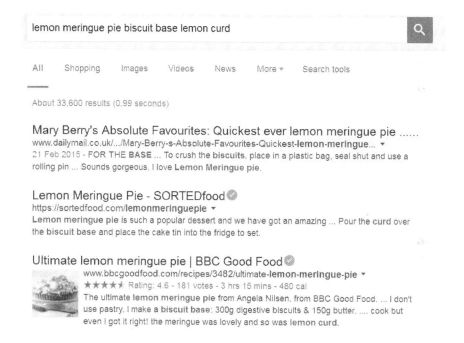

The top three results are still pretty hard to beat but further down the page there are some results you can beat from regular bloggers and foreign websites.

So you want to write about a lemon meringue pie recipe with a biscuit base and lemon curd.

Google isn't like it used to be. You can't simply use the phrase 'lemon meringue pie recipe' over and over again to receive maximum exposure on Google. In fact, Google recognises what you are doing – it's called keyword stuffing - and they will penalise you.

Google is getting ever more intelligent on finding the level of quality an article has. It recognises synonyms for words and also connects words to a theme. See this in action by typing in 'Spanish food' into the Google image search:

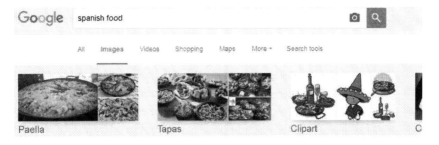

As you can see, words like 'tapas' and 'paella' appear for the search term 'spanish food'. So if you are writing about Spanish food, you have ideas about which other keywords are related to your theme and can be useful. Keywords which are connected to a theme in this way are called LSI keywords. You can get an idea for which LSI keywords connect to your theme with the LSI Graph tool.[1]

For product managers, one keyword tool stands out: soovle.com

At soovle, you can see what people are searching for not just on Google, but answers.com, Wikipedia, Amazon, YouTube, Bing and Yahoo too. You can get keyword ideas to reach people at every stage of the sales funnel, from research (answers.com) to buyer intent (Amazon).

Long tail keywords and long form content

From the example about lemon pie above, you can see how we ended up focusing on a 'long tail keyword' – lemon meringue pie with a biscuit base and lemon curd. We did this because of the competition, but it's also worth noting that people using Google write increasingly descriptive search terms to find what they want. The use of long tail keywords is on the rise.

50% of your keyword focus should be on long tail keywords, according to a study by Statista.[2] It's easy to see why when you see the percentage of long tail searches there are compared to head terms.

To take advantage of this huge amount of long tail search, you need to write long form content. This means more than 2000 words, although some content writers like Neil Patel write more than 3000 words every time they publish an article

Popular Keywords vs. Long Tail Search Traffic

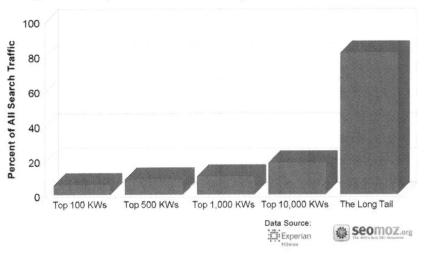

From NeilPatel.com

to give them a bigger advantage.

Writing long form content joins the dots. Google can pick up patterns in your words and knows which ones are related to each other. The more you write in a single article, the more likely it is that you will be picked up. If you wrote an incredibly in-depth article on lemon pie which included a section on biscuit bases, lemon curd, cheesecake and so on, if the searcher types in 'lemon pie cheesecake', you have a chance of appearing in the SERPs *and* if they type in 'lemon pie with a biscuit base', you have a chance too.

Long form content is also a good idea because it provides greater value to the reader. Of course, the content has to be great quality, but presuming it is, readers value in-depth content. An article that barely scratches the surface of a subject is not likely to provide much value or inspire. And if it doesn't inspire, it won't be shared on social media. The statistics back this up:

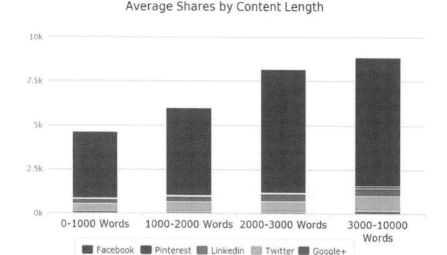

From NeilPatel.com

Sales pages can benefit from more content too. At Vouched-For, we increased our registration page length from merely a form and some copy around it to a long-form page. We saw a conversion improvement of 20%. The startup CrazyEgg tried the same thing and found the same results. People need to know a lot about you and what you offer before they want to invest their time or money.

Targeting the right traffic

If you write about lemon pie for fun, that's fine. Most food bloggers are trying to give their users free and quality information on recipes they love.

But if you're a product manager, you have something to sell.

You are likely writing landing pages or structuring the content on an e-commerce site. If you are a product manager for a cake tin e-commerce company, you will want to target people at every level of the sales funnel.

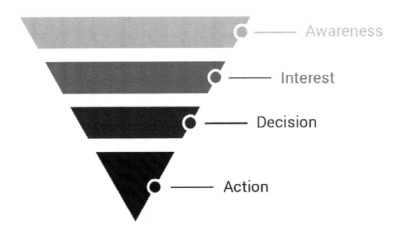

Work with your marketing team on the strategy for reaching people at every stage. You may only work on the e-commerce core site and build landing pages, but your marketing team will be doing a lot of the content marketing work. Your two teams can't work in silos because while it may be two teams, it is one sales funnel.

In the cake tin e-commerce example, it would be right to publish general informative articles on lemon pie because lemon pie is a usage for your cake tin. You can provide people with general information they're looking for in order to reach more people, build brand awareness and build trust. Once you've built enough trust in this way, a site visitor can go from awareness to interest in your product. To make the best lemon pie, they need to buy the best cake tin.

But as well as informative articles, targeting keywords with deeper levels of interest is important too. Here's a table with examples of what I mean:

Interest level	Example keyword to target
Awareness	Lemon pie (or long tail versions of this)
Interest	Cake tin for lemon pie
Decision	Cheap cake tins
Action	Buy cake tin

Competitor research

One important way to know what keywords to target is to see what keywords your competitor is targeting.

SEMRush.com is a great way to do this. You simply type in the name of your competitor and see what keywords they rank for. In the case of cooking equipment, I've chosen te-fal.co.uk.

As you can see, you get a lot of information you can use to decide which keywords to target.

To get an advantage over your competitor, Moz has a great tool to show you the opportunity in a certain keyword area.[3]

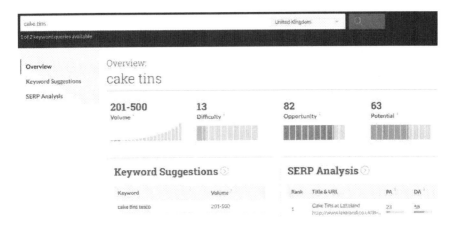

Important places to put your target keyword

There are some places it is important that your target keywords appear:

- In your page title
- In your page's meta description
- In your header tags – h1, h2, h3 (but keep it natural)
- In your page's content
- In your page's URL
- In your image name and alt text (if relevant)
  - Every image should have an 'alt' text. An alt text is what appears to your site visitor if the image fails to load properly so they know what should be there. It also gives Google a good idea of what the image is.

The image alt text can make a real difference in some cases. On an SEO project I was working on, saucydressings.com, when I added an alt text for a picture of paella on a blog about Spanish cuisine, the article received 350% more traffic the next month.

Why user experience matters

Once you've got people to your site, providing great quality content matters. Google's main aim is to give its users relevant and high quality content so it picks up signs from your site activity to judge your site.

Bounce rate and dwell time: if a site visitor comes to one of your pages from Google and then hits the back button, Google knows that your site probably wasn't interesting enough for your user – that's a bounce. But it uses 'dwell' time along with bounce rate to determine relevance because it can be that the bounce rate is high because the visitor got what they were looking for on the first page they came to.[4] Dwell time is the amount of time someone stays on your site.

Relevant external links: linking out to sites with high domain authority which have related pages is a relevance factor for Google. Providing your site visitors with all the information they need provides a better user experience.

Internal links: linking to other relevant pages on your site will reduce your bounce rate and provide your visitor with more relevant information. Having internal links makes it easier for Google to crawl your site and the links themselves are a ranking factor in Google's search algorithm.

Social sharing buttons: despite Google suggesting they don't take social signals into account in their algorithm, being shared on social media makes it more likely for someone to link to you from their website, which Google does care about.[5] There are a few other reasons to add social sharing buttons too:

- Social networks are search engines too
- The obvious, immediate benefit of being shared
- Bing does look at social signals[6]
- If your social buttons have a 'share counter', your page shows greater authority to new site visitors if they can see the page is being shared

Responsive design: as the PageSpeed Insights tool shows, Google can tell if your site is responsively designed for mobile and tablet users and takes other UX factors into account too, like button and font size.

 User Experience

☑ Congratulations! No issues found.

Avoid app install interstitials that hide content
Your page does not appear to have any app install interstitials that hide a significant amount of content. Learn more about the importance of avoiding the use of app install interstitials.

Avoid plugins
Your page does not appear to use plugins, which would prevent content from being usable on many platforms. Learn more about the importance of avoiding plugins.

Configure the viewport
Your page specifies a viewport matching the device's size, which allows it to render properly on all devices. Learn more about configuring viewports.

Size content to viewport
The contents of your page fit within the viewport. Learn more about sizing content to the viewport.

Size tap targets appropriately
All of your page's links/buttons are large enough for a user to easily tap on a touchscreen. Learn more about sizing tap targets appropriately.

Use legible font sizes
The text on your page is legible. Learn more about using legible font sizes.

Some other tips

Page titles are important to get right. In the same way as in a newspaper, you read the headline to decide whether to read the article and the same is true in Google's SERPs. As a general rule, page titles shouldn't be more than 7 words long. At VouchedFor, we used list-based titles, like:

"10 Best Financial Advisers (IFAs) in Twickenham"

As a directory, we had our own search results, which were in a list format. Since it has been proven that people like list-style titles and articles, this worked for us.[7]

Fresh content helps you stay at the top of the Google rankings. Google likes newer content and although some sites try to conceal the published date from Google, it can normally find out.

One slightly risky way to do this is user-generated content – reviews, for example. As Amazon has found out, user-generated content via reviews can lead to fake or humorous

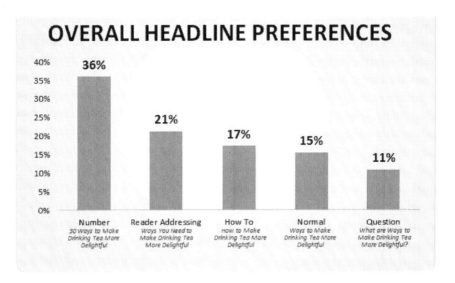

reviews. But at VouchedFor, we were a site run on reviews and our verification methods meant that the review content remained relevant and high quality. The benefits from such content generally hugely outweigh the disadvantages.

Conclusion

SEO is classically a marketing job. But as a product manager, you write the specifications for your website and you can't expect web developers to know SEO. And as a product manager, you need to be able to see the business holistically because the product is linked to every area of the business.

Make your product SEO-friendly and you make it user-friendly. Making it easy to use across all devices and linking to relevant webpages internally and externally – these are things which you should be doing for your users anyway. If you do, your product will have much more success.

25

Introduction to Behavioural Psychology

It's a common phrase in the Product Management world that "you aren't working with products, you're working with people". What that means is that you are working with psychology: what people feel they need, what they feel they want, what they're willing to pay for, what makes them come back to your product, what keeps them focused when using your product. Therefore, to be a successful product manager, you need to understand behavioural psychology.

There are three main parts to basic behavioural psychology: habits; cognitive load; cognitive biases.

Habits

Habits are decisions that used to be conscious but are now automatic. They can be incredibly powerful. One-third of Americans would prefer to give up sex than lose their mobile phones.[1] Enough Japanese men prefer their computers and virtual relationships to real life relationships that it's contributing to Japan's demographic problem.[2] Habits can get you hooked.

If you think this couldn't happen to you, think about how much time you spend on Facebook, Twitter, Farmville (in the old days), Pinterest, Candy Crush or whatever product you use for what you know is far too long. It's no coincidence or necessarily a lack of self-discipline that you are hooked on these products – they've been designed to get you hooked.

Of course, if you are successful at this as a product manager, it can lead you into morally dubious territory. The difference is between persuasion and manipulation. But more on that later. For now, the question is how do we make this work?

The answer is in The Hook Model, designed by Nir Eyal.[3]

It starts off with the **trigger**, which leads to an **action**. The action provides you with a **reward**. Once rewarded, you **invest** something of yourself into the product that makes the process more rewarding in the next cycle.

The Hook Model

Trigger

External

Internal

Action

Investment

Variable
Reward

Courtesy of Nir Eyal, NirAndFar.com

Trigger

A trigger is what makes you want to take an action. Before a habit has been formed, these must come from external sources e.g. a notification on your phone. After a habit has formed, these are ideally internal e.g. I'm feeling lonely (that's the trigger), so I'll go on Facebook for some quick social connection.

Action

The trigger leads you to take an action. With every action we take, we do this in anticipation of a reward. For example, when you type in a question on Google (the action), the reward is to see the answer.

Variable reward

Getting a reward makes you pleased that you took the action. It makes you more likely to do three things: take the action again; take other actions on your product; return the favour – the act of reciprocation e.g. 'if you liked this game, please share it with your friends'.

But if you get the same reward every time you take an action, you are more likely to lose interest. The novelty goes away.

However, if you get a different reward each time you take an action, you are more likely to keep doing it. When you log into Facebook, you see a different post at the top of your newsfeed nearly every time, even if you reload the page after just a minute, for example. The novelty remains and the reward of social connection remains just as strong.

Investment

Investment is about investing in the product with something of yourself – time, money, social capital, data or effort, for example. It's about putting a little bit of 'you' into the product to enhance the experience.

This phase is sometimes misunderstood. There are two parts of it.

The sunk-cost fallacy: the moment you invest something of yourself into a product, that's a cost you've sunk into it. Once you've sunk some cost into a product, you want to keep going at it otherwise you've just wasted your time. By not continuing, you are essentially criticising yourself for your past decisions which, subconsciously, you don't want to do.

Building your own experience: the critical part of this phase. The investment you make in the product should be one that improves your experience of it in the next Hook Cycle. For example, inviting friends on Facebook (the investment) improves your Facebook network, thus improving your experience of the Facebook product.

Once you've gone through all four phases of the cycle, you are on your way to starting a new habit. The next cycle may start with an internal trigger now rather than being reminded to start the new cycle with an external one.

Breaking old habits is hard and creating new ones are just as hard. Often in product management, you are trying to break an old habit of your customers and replace it with a new one, so you will need several cycles before something becomes a habit.

There's no 'normal' timeframe on creating a new habit. It completely depends on your domain, your customers, your product and the habit you are trying to instil.

A hypothetical case study

Let's take the example of FoodZube, the recipe planning and delivery app. The app does all the planning for you – getting the right recipes for your diet, taste and budget and calculating the quantities right for you. It also finds the right supermarket products for your recipes so all you have to do is press the 'Buy' button and your groceries come to your door the next day. If we wanted to create a Hook Cycle for FoodZube, how would we do it?

Trigger

The user gets a push notification or text message saying your next week's recipes have been planned and are ready to buy and be delivered.

Action

The user presses the 'Buy' button and finishes their checkout at the supermarket website. The process is fast and self-explanatory.

Variable reward

The next day, the groceries arrive. Next week, there will be a different set of recipes. This is a variable reward in itself. If your target user is a busy parent who didn't have the time to cook proper meals for their family before FoodZube, the reward may also be bringing the family together for dinner and eating a healthy meal for the first time.

Investment

Once you've cooked your meal, FoodZube will suggest you

write your notes on it so you can cook it even better next time. Over the course of a month, the user will start to build up a hefty recipe collection of their own with notes on dozens of recipes. With each recipe plus notes added to the recipe collection, the user invests more time in their FoodZube experience, enriching it each time.

***

That is just one possible Hook Cycle for the app. Each stage needs testing and researching. If users are using the recipe collection more than the grocery delivery part of the app, for example, you may want to focus your product on that area instead, which may mean an entirely different Hook Cycle.

Cognitive Load

In an ever more distracting world, people have a thousand things on their mind at any one time. As you're reading this, you may be thinking about starting your dinner, what you need to do tomorrow or waiting for a WhatsApp message from a friend. And meanwhile stimuli may be coming from music, your phone, your computer and your TV. People's attention spans have grown smaller in the last 10 years and are now shorter than a goldfish's.[4] It's about 8 seconds on average.

If you think about successful products, the best ones are often the ones with the fewest distractions. **WhatsApp** is so simple you can't miss what you have to do. **Medium** is well-known for its singular focus on their articles. **Twitter** has only the tweets you want to see on your feed – there's nothing on either side of it.

You want to make your product as easy to use as possible with the least amount of focus necessary unless your product is specifically made to be immersive, like a game or a slot-machine. Sometimes you can do this by getting rid of options and sometimes you can do it by setting default options.

To ensure you make the best product for your users, you need research when your users are using your product, what else they have on their mind at the time and in what context are they making decisions about how to use your product.

Cognitive Bias

Cognitive bias is the in-built way our brains work that make us biased for or against a particular option. We have dozens of these, so I'll only go through some of the main ones.

Social proof/consensus

If everyone else is doing it, it must be the right thing to do. That is the basis of the social proof bias. The elevator experiment from the 1960s demonstrates this bias nicely.[5] A TV programme got two of its staff to enter an elevator and face the wall. An oblivious man then walks in and starts to feel the pressure to face the wall too. As more staff from the TV programme enter and face the wall, the pressure increases and the man also slowly turns to face the wall.

In 2008, there was an experiment set up to persuade hotel guests to re-use their towels.[6] This was a classic A/B test. The researchers gave some guests one message and some guests a different message.

The first message focused on environmental concern. It said: "HELP SAVE THE ENVIRONMENT. You can show your respect for nature and help save the environment by reusing your towels during your stay."

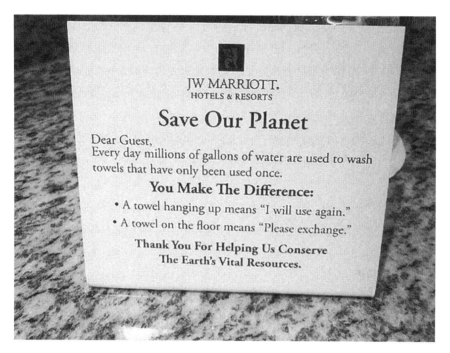

Flickr user Joel Kramer

The second message focused on social consensus. It said: ""JOIN YOUR FELLOW GUESTS IN HELPING TO SAVE THE ENVIRONMENT. Almost 75% of guests who are asked to participate in our new resource savings program do help by using their towels more than once. You can join your fellow guests in this program to help save the environment by reusing your towels during your stay."

The second message outperformed the first 44% participation to 35%.

In a second experiment, researchers referred in their new message to previous guests in that specific hotel room and found an even more positive response.

Lots of products use social proof. Ratings, reviews and testimonials are common ways to take advantage of social proof. AirBnB found reviews completely transformed their business.[7] A consumer study showed that 88% of consumers read customer reviews online before they decided to buy.[8] 85% of customers read up to 10 reviews before they started to trust the business in question.

Another way to harness the power of social proof is to show what other customers have done, as iTunes and Amazon do all the time.

Here's iTunes:

And here's Amazon:

Customers Who Viewed This Item Also Viewed

Beats by Dr. Dre Studio 2.0 Over-Ear Headphones - White	Beats by Dr. Dre Studio 2.0 Over-Ear Headphones - Black	Beats Solo2 Wireless Headphones, Active Collection - Yellow	Beats Solo2 Wireless Headphones, Active Collection - Blue
★★★★☆ 88	★★★★☆ 88	★★★★☆ 37	★★★★☆ 37
£199.99 ✓Prime	£219.00 ✓Prime	£199.00	£199.00

If you are an e-commerce site, having a 'best selling' category can be very helpful.

On SaucyDressings.com, the 'Trending' menu option is consistently the most clicked on option.

And sharing statistics with how many happy users you have or how many people have shared your content is another to leverage social proof. This is on the Shopify blog, for example.

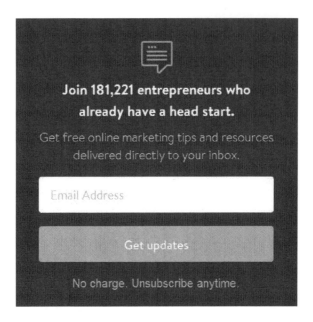

As in the hotel experiment, which referred to previous guests, the more personal the social proof, the better. For example, TripAdvisor lets users who log in with Facebook see where their friends have travelled to and what they would recommend. Showing that your own friends use and like a product makes you more likely to use the product yourself.

Authority

Did you know that Lionel Messi has an endorsement deal with Adidas worth £14m? Anyone can endorse Adidas' products but they'd probably be paid £9 an hour, not £14m. The difference is that Messi is seen as the foremost expert in his field. If Messi says Adidas' products are the best, they probably are – at least, that's the psychology.

If Messi tried to sell parts of ship engines, the sales conversion may still be higher than if he didn't, but potential ship engine customers wouldn't take him as seriously as football fans would because authority is relative to domain.

One way of showing authority is to have a section on your home or landing page which shows high-profile businesses which have used your product or newspapers which have featured your product.

AS FEATURED IN

A generic 'Featured In' section

Smack an 'As featured in' section into almost any landing page and you can make your own brand more trustworthy, results of A/B tests allowing. But make sure to think about which brands are well-known enough to go on your section and which you want to associate your own brand with.

Let users find out more about what the brands said about you to deepen the relationship of trust. Just saying you've been featured somewhere without any further information doesn't add greatly to the authority of your site. For all your site visitors know, the companies who used your service or the newspaper articles could have a negative view of your product. But equally, you wouldn't want to link out to the original article because you want visitors to stay on your site.

Providing extra information in a tool tip, next to the brand logos may work for you.

There are many other ways you can improve the authority of

your site, and a few of these include:

- **Consistent design** is vital.
- **Photos** must look professional. You could be an e-commerce site which needs beautiful photos of products or a directory which needs professional photos of people. Generally, the smarter the photos are, the more authoritative your site will appear. Smiling faces, a head and shoulder shot, and a suit and tie (for a man) all provide high authority.
- **Names** are important. Shopify calls their partners in web design, development and marketing 'Shopify Experts', for example. Apple calls its customer service team 'geniuses'. Names on your website or app can make a difference.
- **An About page** needs to have a lot of thought put into it. A lot of visitors go to the About page as *the* page to know whether to trust you.

Anchoring

Anchoring is where you frame a situation by providing a point of reference for the entire negotiation to come. It's why many salespeople prefer to open negotiations. If I'm selling you a TV and I say the TV cost me £400 when I bought it a year ago, I just anchored negotiations. My aim was always to get you to pay £300, so providing the information above makes it more likely that you will.

There's a great example of this principle from an experiment Dan Ariely did with pricing for the magazine The Economist.

Ariely asked 100 MIT students to choose from different pricing options.[9]

Subscription Type	Yearly cost	Percentage that chose it
Web only	$59	16%
Print only	$125	0%
Print and Web	$125	84%

Ariely then repeated the experiment with two pricing options and a different set of students.

Subscription Type	Yearly cost	Percentage that chose it
Web only	$59	68%
Print and Web	$125	32%

The perceived value of the 'Print and Web' option was much higher when the context of 'Print Only' was provided.

Reciprocity

This is the bias that makes you more likely to do something for someone else if you feel like they have given something to you.

Phillip Kunz, a university professor, once sent out holiday cards to people he had never met.[10] Many recipients sent their own holiday cards with news from their family in return. Some continued to send Mr. Kunz cards years thereafter.

Being the first to offer a favour, especially when none is expected, can lead to reciprocation many times over.

Intercom.io has a feature which tells you users' sign up anniversary. It lets you send an automated message to them on that day so they know they're valued.

Scarcity

You want what you can't have. And you also want something that seems exclusive. It's the reason why nightclubs have queues outside the door even when the club is empty inside.

For its first two years, Pinterest required an invitation before someone was allowed to join the site.

During this period, Pinterest became the fastest-growing site ever, with more than 10 million users in nine months.[11]

Scarcity has a two-fold effect: it makes your product more desirable and injects a sense of urgency. In other words, people want your product and they want it fast. This can lead to viral growth. People share things online and offline with friends to show value. Sharing something you have but others don't increases your own perceived value, and so you are more likely to share it.

Countdown clocks, 'sold out' signs on some products and 'only 2 left in stock' signs on products are some ways of bringing the scarcity principle to life.

Recently, I saw an ad which said:

24 hours left to get "Secret Sauce: A Step-by-step guide to growth hacking" on Kickstarter before parts of the package disappear forever!" This is a great way to use the scarcity principle.

Liking

This is simple: we are more likely to buy from people we like. That could mean someone or something you are attracted to, not just those you have a close social bond with.

Having a site which is enjoyable to use (e.g. beautiful, easy to use, nice animation effects and so forth) can make your customers more likely to buy from you.

Your copy can also make a difference. Lots of sites are using more informal language so they can connect with their customers on a more emotional level. Instead of 'Error: something went wrong', you write 'Well, this is embarrassing'.

 ## Well, this is embarrassing.

Firefox is having trouble recovering your windows and tabs. This is usually caused by

You can try:

* Removing one or more tabs that you think may be causing the problem
* Starting an entirely new browsing session

Having a good idea of who your customers are makes it easier to get the right tone with them and in theory, they'll like you more for it.

As well as tone, complimenting and congratulating your users where appropriate can also get your customers to like you.

UX is a lot about your relationship with your customer so turning your product into something which almost interacts with him or her can grow a bond between your product and your customer.

Loss-aversion – free trials

Have you ever used your credit card instead of the cash in your wallet so the loss of money doesn't feel quite as real? If so, that's your cognitive bias for loss aversion in play.

Studies have shown that people feel loss more than gain. In fact, a loss is valued up to 2.5 times more than an equal sized gain when research was done in money terms.[12]

This principle has been used to great effect by some betting companies like Betfair with their 'Cash Out' feature.[13] This feature lets people take their winnings early (e.g. before the end of the football match) at worse odds than their original bet. The feature has become popular because people felt the risk of losing their money more than the opportunity of gaining more money by waiting until the end of the match.

Conclusion

A neuroscientist called Antonio Damasio did a study on people who had damaged the part of the brain responsible for emotion.[14] These people seemed normal but couldn't feel emotion. When he studied their decision-making, he discovered that this was practically impossible for them. Even a decision as simple as whether to make a cup of tea or coffee would be difficult for them. The lesson is here is this: emotion is at the heart of every decision we make.

Behavioural psychology is one of the bases not just for UX, but also marketing. In product, you will be involved in both so your understanding of it will make your contributions more valuable.

26

Introduction to HTML, CSS and Javascript

As a product manager of digital products, what you are developing is made of code. Everything you dream of is built of code. The more you can understand this code, the more skilled you will be. You will understand developers better and be able to offer more intelligent suggestions. You will be able to estimate the size of a task better. You will be able to understand the possibilities better. Understanding not just code, but code structure and frameworks is important for your job.

There are a variety of languages and principles you will want to learn (I recommend you look up the DRY principle, for example). I want to briefly go through some of the front end ones.

HTML

Everything on the internet is made up of HTML. You can make an entire website just of HTML and it will have that classic '90s style.

Here's one of my favourite HTML-only sites, hmpg.net:

Congratulations!

You have finally reached the end of the internet!
There's nothing more to see, no more links to visit.
You've done it all.
This is the very last page on the very last server at the very far end of the internet.

You should now turn off your computer and go do something useful with the rest of your life. *

Minimalism itself, you could say.

Here's how the page is coded:

```
<html>
<head>
<title>End of the Internet</title>
<script src="http://www.google-analytics.com/urchin.js" type="text/javascript">
</script>
<script type="text/javascript">
_uacct = "UA-422707-2";
urchinTracker();
</script>
</head>
<body>
<p align=center><font size=+4>Congratulations!</font>
<p align=center><b>You have finally reached the end of the internet!</b><br>
There's nothing more to see, no more links to visit.<br>
You've done it all.<br>
```

OK, so not entirely HTML-only, but almost.

What is HTML?

HTML stands for HyperText Markup Language. It is a markup language which uses tags to identify page elements and lets you add text and styling within those elements.

To take the example of the page above, "End of the Internet" is identified as the 'title' of the page, which means that's what appears on your browser's tab as the page title.

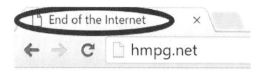

How does it work?

All HTML is inside HTML tags (`<html>` and `</html>`). At the top of the code, there is a header. Every HTML element must have an opening tag (e.g. `<exampletag>`) and a closing tag (e.g. `</exampletag>`).

With the tags, you can add styling e.g. `align=center`, which centres the element. So

`<p align=center>` is the opening tag for a paragraph. This paragraph will be centred by width in the middle of the page.

After the `<head>` comes `<body>`. The header contains data about the page as a whole – this is where you put the `<title>` tag and also where you put CSS styles and Javascript scripts. In HTML5, sometimes the header can be left out altogether.

The body contains the contents of the webpage.

Here are some of the most common HTML tags used:

Tag	Tag meaning
`<h1> - <h6>`	Heading
`<p>`	Paragraph
`<i>`	Italic
`<b>`	Bold
`<a>`	Anchor
`<ul> & <li>`	Unordered List and List Item
`<img>`	Image
`<div>`	Division

You can nest tags inside other tags, like the `<title>` inside the `<head>`. These nested tags are called 'child tags' and the ones they're inside are called parent tags. You must close the child tag before you can close the parent tag.

CSS

CSS is what turned those '90s websites into smart looking ones, like Cinderella going to the ball. It only started being used properly around the year 2000 but even today is notoriously fiddly. When your developer tells you that your simple landing page will take a few days to do, part of the reason will be getting that fiddly CSS right.

What is CSS?

CSS stands for Cascading Style Sheets. HTML structures the page. CSS adds the style and design.

As well as HTML, understanding CSS will be important for you as a product manager because it allows you to play around with the page without the need for a developer to get involved.

Press F12 or right-click and click 'Inspect element' to be able to play around with the styling. You can play around with the fonts, colours, size and position of elements among many other things. If you wondered what that button would look like in red, you can find out here exactly how it would work on the page without distracting a developer.

How does it work?

To add your CSS in HTML, you need to open a `<style>` tag inside the `<head>` tag.

CSS is often added to a CSS file that is linked to from the

HTML file, and can be done inside the `<style>` tag.

That would look like this:

```
<head>
<link rel="stylesheet" type="text/css" href="them
e.css">
</head>
```

But you can also put the CSS directly in the header of your HTML page, and this is known as an 'embedded style'. I've done this when using Mandrill for emails, for example.

Inside the `<style>` tag, your CSS will look like this:

```
h1 {
    color: red;
    text-align: center;
}
```

'h1' refers to the HTML element h1, which you will have within your HTML body below.

Within the curly brackets is what is called the 'declaration block'. Everything within the block styles the HTML element h1 and you can see that you can style the element in more than one way. To style the element in multiple ways, use the semi-colon to split up the different CSS properties.

This covers the barebones basics of CSS. The next most important step for a product manager is to learn the most important CSS properties and how to use them. Ideally, you should be able to style all the elements by yourself.

Javascript

HTML and CSS are all well and good but all they do is show you a page; you can't do anything with it yet. Javascript is what turns a simple set of beautiful pages into a tool. CSS controls the styling of HTML elements; Javascript controls events on your webpage and the behaviour of HTML elements.

How does it work?

All Javascript must be within the HTML tag `<script>`. Like CSS, mostly you will want to put Javascript in an external file and bring it into your webpage as a resource.

When you write your Javascript, you should be aware that it interrupts your page loading. The earlier you have your Javascript in the code, the more likely the important parts of the page won't load as fast as they should.

Like CSS, your script must refer to an HTML element. It does this by 'id'. For example,

```
<button id="bingbong">
```

So this script uses the button I have called 'bingbong' to change the colour of the HTML `<body>` element:

```
<button id="bingbong">

  Click to change text colour

</button>

<script>
```

```
    document.getElementById('bingbong').onclick  =
changeColor;

    var currentColor = "red"

    function changeColor() {

        if(currentColor == "red"){

            document.body.style.color = "green";

            currentColor = "green";

        } else {

            document.body.style.color = "red"

            currentColor = "red"

        }

        return currentColor;

    }
</script>
```

The way this works is simple. It consists of three factors:

- Attach the script to an HTML element
- Trigger the function (the instructions) when a specific event occurs
- Name the function and write the instructions

Here are those factors from the above example:

```
<body>
<h1>I love pineapples</h1>
<p> What else do you want? Pineapples are the answer </p>
<button>click to change colour
</button>
<script>
document.getElementById('bingbong').onclick = changeColor;
var currentColor = "red"
function changeColor() {
if(currentColor == "red"){
document.body.style.color = "green";
currentColor = "green";
} else {
document.body.style.color = "red"
currentColor = "red"
}
return currentColor;
}
</script>
</body>
```

Find HTML element → Event → Function

In the function itself, there is an 'if-else' statement using the variable (var) currentColor.

The variable currentColor is assigned to the colour red using the equals sign. The equals sign (=) assigns a value to a variable.

Where you have a double equals sign (==), the script is checking the value of the variable, rather than assigning it. Essentially, it's asking the question "Is the value of current-Color 'red'?" Only if the answer is yes, will the instructions of what to do if the colour is red apply.

The 'else' part of the function is the instructions for what to do if the colour is not red. The instructions are to make the colour red.

Finally, the 'return' statement makes sure that the variable is updated as the code instructs.

Here's the page this Javascript is on:

I love pineapples

What else do you want? Pineapples are the answer.

Click to change text colour

When you press the button, the header "I love pineapples" and the text "What else do you want? Pineapples are the answer." will change colour from red to green and if you press the button again, the text will go back to red.

You can override styling instructions in Javascript by making specific instructions in CSS for an element. If you had CSS instructions for the h1 text to remain red, for example, on the smaller text would change colour when you press the button.

Conclusion

I wrote this introduction to HTML, CSS and Javascript so you can start to read the code of the product you're building. Your developers will be researching new ways to improve all the time, so you have a lot to catch up on. The world of programming goes deep – languages, frameworks, devices, principles – and a product manager should have a good grip of the basics. Many companies prefer product managers who come from a tech background because they see this understanding as paramount to success in product management, so you can see how important the field is.

Luckily, you won't have to write much code yourself (or any, probably) and you can see from this chapter that these languages work logically and with some training, you can pick up the basics.

Epilogue

In this book, you have learnt the basics of research and design. You have picked up some of the principles and skills vital for product management like behavioural psychology, coding and SEO. You have tips on tools you can use and you've seen how I tackle the daily challenges a product manager faces.

Some say that a product manager is a Jack of all trades and there is some truth in this. You have to understand about marketing, coding, customer service, psychology, design and much more without necessarily being an expert in these fields. But this also means that you can always be a better product manager. There are always new things to learn.

I have provided a short list of books and sites at the end of this book to help you on your way. Some focus on research, some on psychology and some on strategy.

Product managers are the inventors of the future so don't stick rigidly to ideas or structures – be the one to take us where no-one's been before!

Glossary

Acceptance criteria – the conditions set that the code for a backlog task must satisfy to be regarded as complete. These conditions are Boolean – they have a clear pass or fail result. I present these in a Given/When/Then format i.e. *Given some precondition When I do some action Then I expect some result*

Backlog – a backlog is the queue of tasks and features waiting to be built

Backlog grooming – refining your backlog to provide a more realistic picture of what will be done and how long it will take. Typically, tasks will be removed from the backlog, estimates are added to others and more detailed specs. This sometimes happens at a grooming meeting (which I often do informally).

Black-hat SEO – techniques to trick search engines into providing a website a high ranking using dubious means e.g. link farming. The Google search algorithm is very smart these days and will likely pick up what the SEO is trying to do and punish the website with a lower ranking.

Cohort analysis – analysis of a set of users grouped by the time they signed up. I normally do this by month. If you use the right metrics, cohort analysis can show you the progress of your app more accurately than raw numbers of sign ups or paying members, for example.

Deployment – a deployment is a release of code from one site environment to another. For example, a developer may release code from his local machine to your staging site – that process is a deployment.

Kanban – a software development process that prioritises continuous development. Developers start on the next highest priority tasks as they gain the capacity to do so. The developer sees the task through to completion (i.e. releasing their code to the live environment and successfully completing post-release testing) before starting on the next task.

Live environment – your live website/app that your real users use (also known as production).

OKRs – stands for 'Objectives and Key Results', they're similar to KPIs (Key Performance Indicators). They are essentially your business goals and the key metrics you need to focus on to reach those goals.

Pair programming – two developers working at the same computer; taking turns, one writes the code while the other reviews it.

Pull request – a request by a developer to add the code he or she has just written to the team's Git repository. Other members of the development team can review the changes, discuss them and decide whether to accept the request in the current form.

QA – stands for 'quality assurance'. QA merely refers to the methods used to ensure high quality software. People sometimes refer to a testing/staging environment as QA because that's where code is testing for quality. Some companies have QA teams separate from the developers, who test the quality of the code written by the developers.

Regression testing – testing core app functionality after a release of new code. You can do regression testing on a staging or live environment. Ideally, this is mostly done automatically using a browser and device emulator like BrowserStack.

Sprint – a software development work cycle, normally completed in one or two weeks. Design teams like to follow the same model and use 'Design Sprints'.

User stories – software task descriptions which focus on the user. They explain who the task is for, what they want and why they want it. They normally look like this: *As a [user type], I want to [do an action/task] so that [motivation].*

Further Reading

The Lean Startup by Eric Ries

Hooked by Nir Eyal

Lean UX by Jeff Gothelf and Josh Seiden

The Mom Test by Rob Fitzpatrick

Intercom on Jobs-To-Be-Done

The (Honest) Truth About Dishonesty by Dan Ariely

NeilPatel.com – Neil's in-depth articles on marketing and product

Everything on MindTheProduct.com

References

Chapter 2 – Product: Strategy: The Basis of Every Decision

1. Trello is an incredibly simple project management tool. It's free. Learn more at Trello.com

Chapter 3 – Understanding Your Customers

1. Joe Gabbia talks a lot about AirBnB's growth. His TED talk is worth a watch. Here is him on talking to his customers: http://www.cbsnews.com/news/airbnbs-joe-gebbia-forget-about-scale-go-talk-to-your-customers/

Chapter 4 – Research Techniques

1. EA's uplift: http://blog.hubspot.com/marketing/a-b-testing-experiments-examples#sm.0000m4zsrz5wdd5ivls1alw6kuuw8

Chapter 5 – UX Design: The Basics

1. Every second counts: http://www.aberdeen.com/research/5136/ra-performance-web-application/content.aspx

Chapter 6 – Minimum Viable Products: Where It All Starts

1. Dropbox's MVP video:
   https://www.youtube.com/watch?v=xy9nSnalvPc
2. Minimum Loveable Products: https://medium.com/the-happy-startup-school/beyond-mvp-10-steps-to-make-your-product-minimum-loveable-51800164ae0c#.krjlpcwal

Chapter 7 – UX Design: Further Points

1. On why we like rounded corners:
   http://uxmovement.com/thinking/why-rounded-corners-are-easier-on-the-eyes/
2. How to deal with loading screens:
   http://blog.usabilla.com/how-to-integrate-waiting-time-user-experience/
3. Font sizes in desktop:
   https://developers.google.com/speed/docs/insights/Use LegibleFontSizes and sizes in mobile:
   https://blogs.adobe.com/creativecloud/xd-essentials-typography-in-mobile-apps/
4. UX for dyslexic users:
   http://uxmovement.com/content/6-surprising-bad-practices-that-hurt-dyslexic-users/
5. Serif vs sans serif experiments:
   https://www.usertesting.com/blog/2014/08/06/choosing-the-right-font-a-guide-to-typography-and-user-experience/
6. Why using 'optional' fields can be better:
   http://uxmovement.com/forms/why-users-fill-out-less-if-you-mark-required-fields/

Chapter 9 – Transitioning to Continuous Development

1. The project management software I use most often: https://www.atlassian.com/software/jira

Chapter 13 – Feature Bloat: Why Features Sometimes Aren't The Answer

1. How WhatsApp became successful with a low employee count: http://www.mindtheproduct.com/2014/02/whatsapp-power-product-focus/

Chapter 14 – Time Management

1. Raygun – a great tool to track site errors: Raygun.com

Chapter 16 – Your Product Roadmap

1. Gov.uk's roadmap: http://cdn02.mindtheproduct.com/wp-con-tent/uploads/2014/07/Roadmap.10.07.14_redact.pdf

Chapter 17 – How To Prioritise Product Development

1. Why small requests can be a red herring: https://blog.intercom.io/first-rule-prioritization-no-

snacking/

Chapter 19 – Google Analytics: The Basics

1. Optimizely is the current market leader in A/B testing. It's easy to learn. Optimizely.com
2. How to set up Google Analytics events: https://support.google.com/analytics/answer/1136960?hl=en

Chapter 20 – Intercom: Your Secret Weapon

1. Segment – a tool that has a lot of potential. Although we didn't manage to make it work for us, I'll definitely experiment with it in the future. Having all your data go through one gateway makes things easy. See more at segment.com

Chapter 21 – SEO: An Introduction

1. Monster Insights Google Analytics plugin: https://wordpress.org/plugins/google-analytics-for-wordpress/

Chapter 22 – Technical SEO

1. Subdomains can cause a problem: https://moz.com/blog/subdomains-vs-subfolders-rel-canonical-vs-301-how-to-structure-links-optimally-for-seo-whiteboard-friday

2. Always see if a page is noindex:
   https://chrome.google.com/webstore/detail/seerobots/h
   nljoiodjfgpnddiekagpbblnjedcnfp?hl=en
3. Google on nofollow:
   http://www.shoutmeloud.com/understand-dofollow-
   nofollow-link-seo-basics.html

Chapter 23 – Off-page SEO

1. One of the most comprehensive lists of Google's ranking factors: http://backlinko.com/google-ranking-factors
2. The 80/20 principle is one of the most important principles to live by in Product Management. For example, it stops you prioritising edge cases that won't help your business really move forward: https://en.wikipedia.org/wiki/Pareto_principle
3. Moz's super useful SEO toolbar: https://moz.com/tools/seo-toolbar
4. Guest blogging's dubious status with Google: https://www.quicksprout.com/2014/01/22/guest-blogging-and-seo-still-a-match-made-in-heaven/
5. Pat Flynn's backlinking strategy: http://www.smartpassiveincome.com/backlinking-strategy-2014-beyond/
6. Google's widget guideline: http://searchengineland.com/official-googles-latest-official-stance-on-links-within-widgets-181475

Chapter 24 – On-page SEO

1. http://lsigraph.com/
2. Why you should focus on long-tail keywords:

http://www.statista.com/statistics/267516/search-engine-optimization-for-long-tail-keywords/

3. Moz's Explorer tool: https://moz.com/explorer
4. Dwell time: http://backlinko.com/on-page-seo
5. Google say they don't use social signals in their search algorithm: https://www.youtube.com/watch?v=udqtSM-6QbQ
6. Bing does use social signals: https://blog.kissmetrics.com/social-media-and-seo/
7. List form content in SEO: http://neilpatel.com/2015/09/17/creating-content-that-converts-the-step-by-step-guide/

Chapter 25 – Introduction To Behavioral Psychology

1. Mobile phones greater than sex? One-third of Americans seem to think so: http://www.telenav.com/about/pr-summer-travel/report-20110803.html
2. Japan's virtual relationship problem: http://www.bbc.com/news/magazine-24614830
3. *Hooked: How To Build Habit-Forming Products* by Nir Eyal (New York: Portfolio Penguin, 2014)
4. Low attention spans: http://www.telegraph.co.uk/science/2016/03/12/humans-have-shorter-attention-span-than-goldfish-thanks-to-smart/
5. The elevator experiment: https://www.youtube.com/watch?v=BgRoiTWkBHU
6. The hotel towel experiment: http://www.fastcodesign.com/3037679/evidence/read-about-how-hotels-get-you-to-reuse-towels-everyones-doing-it
7. Joe Gabbia's TED talk:

https://www.ted.com/talks/joe_gebbia_how_airbnb_de
signs_for_trust

8. Consumers care about online reviews:
    https://www.brightlocal.com/learn/local-consumer-
    review-survey-2014/

9. Dan Ariely's anchoring experiment:
    http://www.ted.com/talks/dan_ariely_asks_are_we_in_
    control_of_our_own_decisions?language=en

10. Philip Kunz's holiday card experiment:
    http://www.npr.org/sections/health-
    shots/2012/11/26/165570502/give-and-take-how-the-
    rule-of-reciprocation-binds-us

11. Pinterest was the fastest growing site ever:
    http://www.bbc.com/news/technology-19197531

12. Losses feel bigger than gains:
    http://www.youthareawesome.com/losses-loom-larger-
    than-gains/

13. The Betfair ad:
    https://www.youtube.com/watch?v=qtIEOe7CRT0

14. *Descartes' Error: Emotion, Reason and the Human
    Brain* by Antonio Damasio (New York: Avon Books,
    1994).

ABOUT THE AUTHOR

Thomas Raffael has been building online products for the last five years, from online newspapers to fintech apps. He lives in London and Hamburg.

Printed in Great Britain
by Amazon